Joseph Bucklin

Cheap-Money Experiments in Past and Present Time

Reprinted with slight revision

Joseph Bucklin

Cheap-Money Experiments in Past and Present Time
Reprinted with slight revision

ISBN/EAN: 9783744727006

Printed in Europe, USA, Canada, Australia, Japan

Cover: Foto ©Suzi / pixelio.de

More available books at **www.hansebooks.com**

CHEAP-MONEY EXPERIMENTS

IN PAST AND PRESENT TIMES

REPRINTED, WITH SLIGHT REVISION, FROM
"TOPICS OF THE TIME" IN
THE CENTURY MAGAZINE

NEW YORK
THE CENTURY CO.
1892

CONTENTS

CHEAP-MONEY EXPERIMENTS IN PAST AND PRESENT TIMES

CHAPTER I

THE PEOPLE AND FINANCE

THERE are a few elementary principles in economic science the mastery of which by the great body of the American people would be of incalculable value to us as a nation. One of these is that no government can create money out of anything which it may choose to call money. Another is that all classes of the people, rich and poor, laborer and employer, are far better off with a sound and stable currency than they are with any of the varieties of "cheap money." Another is that no part of the financial or business world can be benefited or injured by changes in the monetary standard of value without corresponding benefit or injury to the other parts. Still another is that the larger part of the business of the country is transacted upon credit, and that anything which tends to disturb or to foreshadow

disturbances of the monetary standard of value
cripples credit and demoralizes all business. Finally, though we have by no means exhausted the
list, it would be of the highest importance for the
common people to become thoroughly convinced
of the fact that in every instance in which the
financial world is disturbed by changes or threats
of changes in the standard of value the sufferers
are always the poorer people and the beneficiaries
always the rich, for the latter are able to guard
against the coming trouble which they are quick
to scent, while the former are powerless to take
the necessary precautions even if they were able
to anticipate it.

The harmful delusion that the Government has
the power to create money is traceable directly to
the Legal Tender Act of 1862. Previous to that
time the American people, in common with those
of other enlightened nations, believed that the sole
function of government in relation to money was
to certify to the weight and purity of the metal
contained in it. This view, which, it is scarcely
necessary to say, has been shown by the experience of all civilized countries to be the only sound
one, was completely upset in the minds of thousands of uninstructed people by the issue of the
legal tenders and the subsequent decisions of the
Supreme Court upholding the right of Congress
to make such issue. The pernicious doctrine that
anything which the Government might choose to
stamp as money—paper, or silver, or nickel, or

copper — became *ipso facto* money for the amount named on its face obtained so firm a lodgment in the popular mind that calls began to be heard from all quarters for the liberal issue of Government money in almost every form except — gold. The country has passed safely through several varieties of the " greenback craze," which was the most radical and dangerous form of the delusion, but it has yet to reach the solid ground occupied before the war. So long as the admission is allowed that the Government can create money there is no satisfactory answer to be made to the questions, "Why should we have a gold standard?" "Why should we have national banks?" or "Why should we have any limit put to the volume of our currency?" If the Government can create money, why should it not create all that everybody wants? Why should anybody work for a living?

We must get back as a people to a just comprehension of the truth that no government can make an inferior form of money equal in value to a superior form like gold by enacting a law decreeing that it shall become so, and that it cannot do this for the simple reason that the superior form costs more, and it is this cost which constitutes its value as a medium of exchange. The kind of money which every man wants is the kind which will buy the most of the things which he needs — that is, have the largest purchasing power. Nothing is clearer than that cheap money means high prices, and dear money means low prices. Cheap money is as costly for a nation as it is for an individual. Mr. H. C. Adams has demonstrated very convincingly that the legal tenders made the expense of our civil war greater by $800,000,000 than it would have been had they never been issued. With individuals, the only man who is benefited by a change from a dear money to a cheaper one is he who owes money — that is, belongs to what is called the debtor class. He is rid at once of a portion of his debt, because he can pay it in money of less value than that in use at the time of the debt's contraction. But to the average man, the wage-earner of every variety, the change means greatly increased cost of living with no increase of income. He still receives the same number of dollars as wages, but each dollar buys less than it did before. If he has debts, the depreciation of them is by no means in the same proportion as in his wages. Suppose, for example, he is receiving $1000 a year and that he owes $1000. A reduction of ten per cent. in the value of money means that his wages have been cut down one tenth — that is, that he will lose $100 each year, whereas his debt has only been reduced $100 for all time.

The people who would benefit at first by a change to cheap money are farmers and others who have property which is heavily mortgaged, and who would be thus relieved of a portion of their debt. The case of the farmer who has been forced to mortgage his farm is a peculiarly hard one. His condition has been growing worse and worse yearly, for many reasons, but chiefly because most of the things he has had to buy have been taxed, while the chief products of his farm have not. He has been forced to buy at the higher prices of a restricted home market, and to sell at the prices set in the unrestricted market of the world. A change to a cheaper form of money would give him relief, provided he were able to pay off his debt at once, but otherwise his gain would be only in his ability to pay his interest money in a cheaper currency. He would suffer, in common with all others of the hard-working class, from the inevitable evils attendant upon cheap money, with the dear goods which such money always brings in its train. Then, too, he would discover, in case he wished to procure further loans, that he must obtain them on a gold basis, for the mere hint of the coming of a cheaper currency is sufficient always to force capitalists into the defensive position of loaning large amounts on that basis alone. In the end the farmer would find that his last condition was worse than his first, and that his every effort to gain relief through legislation which promised to make "money plenty" had the same result,— namely, to put him more helplessly in the power of men whose chief business is to speculate in money.

Another class of temporary beneficiaries from cheaper money are employers, who are able to pay their employees in the cheap money, in small amounts, at its full nominal value, while obtaining it for such payment in large amounts and at its gold value. Yet we believe it is a fact that the great body of employers are agreed that the slight gains which are possible in this way are far from being an adequate set-off to the losses caused to all business by the uncertainties of an unstable currency. Another class is composed of the professional speculators in gold and the hoarders of gold, who, because of their possession of capital, are able to speculate in the superior money at the expense of the great mass of the people, who are compelled to accept the inferior medium of exchange.

All this leads naturally and inevitably to the general conclusion that the best money for all classes in the long run — of course, including the farmers — is that which is most stable in value; that is, which most completely and steadily serves the purpose of a medium of exchange. It should be constantly borne in mind that the great volume of the business of the country, what is called exchange of commodities, is conducted on credit. Statistics show that about ninety-two per cent. of the trade of the country is carried on by means of credit instruments and only eight per cent. with actual money. The mere hint of a change in the value of money sends a thrill of alarm along the entire credit system, and leads to instantaneous contraction. This is at once felt in every branch of business and industry. There is at once a double strain put upon the trade of the country.

Gold and currency are hoarded in anticipation of approaching uncertainty of values, and credit is given only in cases of the strongest security. All our serious commercial troubles, our panics and threatened panics, our tight money-markets and business stringencies, are directly traceable to this contraction of credit; yet the uninstructed public almost invariably calls for the issue of cheaper money as the only remedy, not recognizing that the mischief has been caused, not by a scarcity of currency, but by a contraction of credit.

There ought to be a more general recognition of the fact that the economic administration of a nation, the regulation of its currency and finances, calls for expert ability of a rare kind. In every generation there are comparatively few men who have the requisite intellectual equipment for this task, and in almost every other civilized country except ours they are sought out and put in exclusive charge of it. Few intelligent people venture upon the experiment of being their own doctors or lawyers, recognizing the superior fitness of expert ability to perform those functions. Why shall we as a nation be less wise? We must sooner or later realize the folly of our course, and must devise some plan, not inconsistent with the principles of popular government, by which the control of our finances shall be put into the hands of a few tried and trained financiers, who shall be removed absolutely beyond the influence of popular clamor. We shall then have far less trouble than we have now. The people at large would be benefited in every way, and in none more so than through the restrictions which such administration of our finances would put upon the activities of certain conscienceless manipulators in Wall street, who find now their best opportunities for mischief in the uncertainty which constant meddling with the standard of value inevitably produces.

CHAPTER II

THE ENGLISH LAND BANK

THE desire for "cheap money," under the delusion that plenty of it will make everybody's life easier and his burdens lighter, is very many years old. Nothing is more interesting and instructive in the study of financial history than the almost constant recurrence of the same fallacies and popular crazes in different countries during the past three hundred years or more. The prophets of new panaceas of to-day are simply preaching the half-truths and misleading sophistries of similar prophets in various lands at almost any time since the close of the seventeenth century. They have all started from the same general point; that is, dissatisfaction with established financial methods and the assumption that the moneyed classes, the brokers and capitalists, are the enemies and oppressors of the poorer classes.

There are many illustrations to support these observations which we might cite from history, but none which bears more directly upon certain aspects of our financial experience as a nation than that of the famous Land Bank scheme, put forward in England in the reign of William and Mary, in 1693. It appeared amid a swarm of other financial plans which were broached in the English Parliament when the proposition to establish the Bank of England was under consideration. There were in existence at that time two great public banks renowned throughout Europe, the Bank of St. George at Genoa, and the Bank of Amsterdam. The former had existed for nearly three hundred years, and the latter for more than eighty, and both had demonstrated many times their ability to withstand the severest financial crises. England felt the need of a similar financial bulwark, and its establishment was decreed in 1694, when the act of foundation for the Bank of England was passed by Parliament. While that act was under consideration, one Hugh Chamberlain, who had fitted himself for the solving of financial problems by practising medicine, came forward with a scheme for a Land Bank. The peculiarity of this bank was that its currency was to consist solely of notes issued in unlimited quantities upon landed security. Every person who had real property was to be allowed to hold the land and at the same time receive an issue of paper money to its full value. Thus, says Macaulay, in his picturesque account of the scheme, if a man's "estate was worth two thousand pounds, he ought to have his estate and two thousand pounds in paper money." But this was not all. He ought also to be allowed to rate the value of his estate at as many times its annual income as the number of years for which it was pledged. Thus if its income was a thousand dollars, a grant of it for twenty years must be worth $20,000 in paper money, and that for one hundred years $100,000. Everybody who opposed this remarkable form of reasoning was denounced as a "usurer." In laying his plan before Parliament, Chamberlain undertook to raise eight thousand pounds upon every freehold estate of one hundred and fifty pounds a year, which would be brought into his bank without dispossessing the freeholder. The plan was considered in committee and was reported favorably to the House, the committee declaring that it was practicable and would tend to benefit the nation; but the report was never acted upon.

The scheme was revived in 1696, but in a somewhat less ridiculous form. Chamberlain was forced, under protest, to abandon his idea that a lease of land for a term of years was worth many times the fee simple, and to be content with a bank which lent money on landed security to the full value of the land. He offered also to lend the Government, in return for the Land Bank's charter, more than two and a half million pounds at seven per cent. The Bank of England had, in return for its charter, advanced to the Government only one million at eight per cent. William, being in pressing need of money for his military operations in the Netherlands, welcomed the prospect of such generous aid, and was not disposed to question the source from which it came. The country members were, according to Macaulay, "delighted by the prospect of being able to repair their stables, replenish their cellars, and give portions to their daughters," and at the same time retain possession of their land. A bill was passed authorizing the Government to borrow two million five hundred and sixty-four thousand pounds at seven per cent. If before the 1st of August the subscription for one half of this loan should have been filled, and one half of the sum subscribed should have been paid into the exchequer, the subscribers were to become a corporate body under the name of the National Land Bank. As this bank was intended expressly to accommodate country gentlemen, it was forbidden to lend money on any other private security than a mortgage on land, and must lend on such mortgages at least half a million annually, at a rate not to exceed three and a half per cent. if payments were quarterly, or four per cent. if they were half-yearly. The market rate of interest at the time on the best mortgages was full six per cent.

In order to set a good example the king subscribed five thousand pounds just before his departure on his Netherland campaign, and signed a warrant appointing commissioners to receive the names of subscribers. A great meeting was held in behalf of the new bank, rooms were taken in two different parts of London for the receiving of subscriptions, and agents were sent into the country to inform the country gentlemen of the dawn of the new era of prosperity. Three weeks passed after the opening of the subscription books, and it was discovered that only six thousand five hundred pounds, including the king's five thousand, had been subscribed. The 1st of August came, and the whole amount subscribed by the nation in addition to the king's subscription reached only two thousand one hundred pounds. The promoters of the scheme begged the Government for more time, and for a reduction in the amount required to be paid in before the act of incorporation should be issued; and the Government, being in great stress for funds, conceded that if four hundred thousand pounds were advanced the bank should be incorporated at the next session of Parliament. But concessions were of no avail in stimulating subscriptions. The term of the commission expired, and the offices were closed upon a total collapse of the enterprise.

The causes of this failure are so clear that it is a wonder anybody ever expected a different result. The avowed object of the scheme was to benefit the landowners who wished to borrow money, and to injure the "moneyed men, those worst enemies of the nation." "The fact is," says Professor Thorold Rogers, in his luminous account of the affair in his "First Nine Years of the Bank of England," "the landed men hated the moneyed men with a bitterness in which envy, contempt,

pride, and religious bigotry were the strongest
ingredients. They looked on their growing wealth
with envy, on their occupation with scorn, on their
birth with disdain, on their creed and discipline
with intolerant hate. Now in such a frame of
mind such people will believe anything, even such
a quack as Chamberlain was—not the first adventurer who has imagined himself a financier." Yet
upon these very moneyed men they depended absolutely for the success of their enterprise. As
Macaulay says, the "country gentlemen wished
well to the scheme; but they wished well to it because they wanted to borrow money on easy terms;
and, wanting to borrow, they of course were not
able to lend it. The moneyed class alone could
supply what was necessary to the existence of the
Land Bank; and the Land Bank was avowedly
intended to diminish the profits, to destroy the
political influence, and to lower the social position
of the moneyed class. As the usurers did not
choose to take on themselves the expense of putting down usury, the whole plan failed in a manner
which, if the aspect of public affairs had been less
alarming, would have been exquisitely ridiculous."

There have been within the past year several
schemes for the relief and benefit of the farmers of
the country which were scarcely more rational than
this of the quack of 1693. If any of them were to
be embodied in law, it would fail to accomplish
the results expected of it, for reasons similar to
those which made the failure of the Land Bank

scheme so certain. The moneyed class is always
in the position to guard itself against the bad effects of disturbing financial legislation, and even
to profit by it at the expense of the poorer class.
A competent authority upon the subject of farm
mortgages declares that ninety per cent. of them
are negotiated by systematic lenders, banks, and
corporations organized for this express purpose,
and that it has been the custom of many of these
lenders to make the mortgage debt, both principal
and interest, payable in gold.   It is believed that
fully one half of all the mortgage indebtedness of
the country is in terms expressly payable in gold,
though this is more generally the case in urban
than in farm loans. If we were to have free silver
coinage, and the country were to reach the silver
standard, and gold were to rise to one hundred
and twenty or thereabouts, mortgagers who are
counting upon having their debts reduced by the
change would soon discover their error.   They
would find that they would have to pay one hundred and twenty dollars in silver for every instalment of one hundred dollars interest in gold.   In
other words, they, and not the capitalists and
money-lenders, would be the losers from this as
from every other form of "cheap money."

CHAPTER III

THE RHODE ISLAND PAPER BANK

AT the close of the Revolutionary War the people of Rhode Island found themselves in extreme poverty and heavily burdened with their share of the national debt. The war had seriously crippled their trade, upon which they were mainly dependent, and in their distress the people, instead of patiently waiting for relief to come by the slow process of rebuilding their trade, turned to paper money for relief. They began to clamor for a Paper Bank in 1785, and when petitions for such a bank were rejected by the General Assembly, a new party was organized with paper money as its chief principle. They went before the Assembly again in 1786, and their petitions for a Paper Bank were met with counter-petitions against it, signed by the merchants of Providence, and the project was defeated again by a vote of two to one. They then carried the question into the elections, and won a surprising victory, gaining control of the General Assembly by a large majority. This body assembled in May,

1786, and one of its first acts was the passing of a law establishing a Paper-money Bank of one hundred thousand pounds. The bills were to be loaned to the people on the principle of the English Land Bank, though on much less generous terms.

Every farmer or merchant who came to borrow money must pledge real estate for double the amount desired. The money was to be loaned to the people upon this pledge according to the apportionment of the last tax, and must be paid into the treasury at the end of fourteen years. Great expectations were entertained by the farmers of the beneficent results which were to follow upon this new influx of wealth. " Many from all parts of the State," says McMaster, in a very interesting chapter upon this subject in his " History of the People of the United States," " made haste to avail themselves of their good fortune, and mortgaged fields strewn thick with stones and covered with cedars and stunted pines for sums such as could not have been obtained for the richest pastures. They had, however, no sooner obtained the money and sought to make the first payment at the butcher's or the baker's than they found that a heavy discount was taken from the face-value."

The depreciation of the new money began literally with its issue. Every merchant and tradesman in the State refused to receive it for its face-value, and the holders of it refused to make any discount. The General Assembly came to the aid of the bank, and sought to give its paper money full value by statutory enactment. A forcing act was passed subjecting any person who should refuse to take the bills in payment for goods on the same terms as specie, or should in any way discourage their circulation on such terms, to a fine of one hundred pounds and to the loss of his rights as a freeman.

This made matters worse than ever. Merchants and traders refused to make any sales whatever, many of them closing their shops, disposing of their stock by barter, and going out of business. In fact, money almost ceased to circulate at all. Nearly all kinds of business were transacted by barter, rents were paid in grain and other commodities, and the only people who used the paper money were those who had borrowed it on their land. The chief cities of the State, Providence and Newport, presented a very remarkable spectacle. Half their shops were closed, their inhabitants idle, and their streets animated only by groups of angry and contentious men blaming one another for the blight which had fallen upon their business and industries. In order to retaliate upon the merchants and traders for refusing to take their money, the farmers refused to bring their produce to market. A famine was so imminent in Providence because of this withholding of supplies that a town meeting was called to devise means for obtaining the necessaries of life. To provide immediate relief for persons in want of bread five hundred dollars was authorized to be

borrowed and sent abroad to buy corn to be sold
or bartered by the town council. In Newport a
mob brought on a riot by attempting to force
grain-dealers to sell corn for paper-money.

In August, about two months after the establishment of the bank, affairs became so desperate that
a State convention controlled by the country towns
adopted a report recommending the General Assembly to enforce and amend the penal laws in
favor of paper money, and advising farmers to
withhold their produce from the opponents of the
bank. The General Assembly, convened in special
session for the purpose, passed an additional forcing act, which suspended the usual forms of justice
in regard to offenders against the bank, by requir-
ing an immediate trial, within three days after complaint was entered, without a jury and before a
court of which three judges should constitute a
quorum, whose decision should be final, and whose
judgment should be instantly complied with on penalty of imprisonment. The fine for the first offense
was fixed at from six to thirty pounds, and for the
second at from ten to fifty pounds. "This mon-
strous act of injustice," says S. G. Arnold, in his
"History of the State of Rhode Island," "was
carried through the legislature by a large majority,
and the solemn protest against it as a violation of
every principle of moral and civil right, of the
charter, of the articles of confederation, of treaty
obligations, and of every idea of honor or honesty
entertained among men," which a minority of the

3

members presented, was not allowed to appear on the record.

This second forcing act brought matters to a crisis. A butcher in Newport was brought into the Superior Court on a charge of refusing to receive paper money at par in payment for meat. A great concourse of spectators attended the trial, which was before a full bench of five judges. Leading lawyers appeared for both sides, and their arguments occupied an entire day. Two of the judges spoke against the forcing acts, and the other three were of the same mind. On the following morning the formal decision of the court was announced, declaring the acts unconstitutional and void, and dismissing the complaint. The wrath of the General Assembly at this decision was great. A special session was at once convened, and the judges were summoned, in language of incredible arrogance, to appear before the Assembly to assign the "reasons and grounds" for their decision. Three of the judges obeyed the summons, but as the other two were detained by sickness the hearing was postponed till the next session. At the next session four of the offending judges were removed. Before adjourning, the General Assembly prepared a new act to "stimulate and give efficacy to the paper bills." This was called the Test Act, and it contained one of the most remarkable oaths ever prescribed to a free people. Every one taking the oath bound himself in the most solemn manner to do his ut-

most to support the paper bank and to take its
money at par. All persons refusing to take the
oath were disfranchised. Ship-captains were forbidden to enter or to go out of ports of the State,
lawyers were not to be allowed to practise, men
were not to be allowed to vote, politicians were
not to be allowed to run for office, and members
of the legislature were not to be allowed to take
their seats until the oath had been taken. This
was so stringent a measure that the General Assembly was afraid to take the responsibility of
enacting it, and, after considering it, referred it
to the people of the towns for approval. Only
three towns in the State voted in its favor, all the
others rejecting it.

This ended all efforts to force the people to take
the money at par in ordinary business transactions.
The General Assembly, in January, 1787, formally
repealed the forcing acts, and then took the first
step toward the repudiation of the State debt by
ordering the treasurer to pay off one fourth of it
in the bills received for taxes; that is, in the depreciated paper money, which, at that time, was
circulating on the basis of six to one. By suc-
cessive steps of this and similar kinds the entire
State debt was extinguished, public creditors being
forced to take it on terms prescribed by the State,
or to forfeit their claims. The last instalment of
the debt was got rid of in 1789, in a forced settle-
ment, when the paper money which the helpless
creditors received was worth only one twelfth as

much as coin. "Had a general act of insolvency," says Arnold, "relieving all debtors from their liabilities and the State from its legal obligations been passed in the first instance, the same end would have been more speedily accomplished, and the means would not have differed very widely from those that were actually employed. . . . It fell but little short of repudiation."

During 1787, when the value of the paper money ranged from one sixth to one tenth that of coin, bills in equity for the redemption of mortgaged estates were filed in large numbers in the courts. The Superior Court of Newport declined to try any case in which a large sum was involved. Suitors came to court with paper money in handkerchiefs, bags, and pillow-cases, asking to have the holders of their mortgages forced to take this at par in redemption of their lands. One bag, containing fourteen thousand dollars, was brought for the redemption of a single farm. But the court refused to try all cases of the kind. The value of the paper money dropped steadily till fifteen paper dollars were worth only one coin dollar. In August, 1789, the General Assembly showed its first sign of returning reason by suspending the operation of the tender law. It followed this by repealing the statute of limitations, because of the depreciation in the value of paper money, and by extending the time allowed for the redemption of mortgages from five to twelve years. Finally, in October, it

repealed as much of the Paper Bank act as made
the bills a tender at par, and debtors were authorized to substitute property, at an appraised value,
for money in discharge of debts. The act which
effected the repeal fixed the value of the paper
bills at fifteen to one. This was the end.

Throughout this entire struggle to make money
valuable by statute, by calling it a dollar and saying that it represented two dollars' worth of land,
the bills had remained almost exclusively in the
hands of their first takers. No one else was found
who would receive the money, save those whom
the State compelled to take it, or to forfeit their
just claims. Absolutely nobody had benefited by
the experiment except the State, which had got
rid of a large portion of its debt by dishonestly refusing to keep its obligations. Industry and trade
of all kinds, as well as the State's good name, had
suffered incalculable injury, and the State's material progress had been retarded so seriously that
it required many years to regain what had been
lost. The deluded people who borrowed of the
bank on their land as collateral realized their desire of having more money in their pockets; they
realized the dream, cherished by the believers in
"cheap money" in all lands and at all times, of a
larger *per capita* currency in which they should
share, but they very soon found out that none of
the blessings which they had so fondly imagined
would follow possession were destined to .appear.
What was gained by having plenty of money if it

could not be used in payment of debts, if nothing could be bought with it save at greatly advanced prices, and if it were to become less and less valuable as time went on ?

They began their experiment with a firm belief that they could compel capitalists to share their wealth with them by exchanging their hated dear money for their own cheap money on equal terms, but they soon discovered that all the power of a State government, exerted with unscrupulous zeal, was not sufficient to compel a man to employ his capital in ways against his will. They might prevent him from collecting usury, but they could not interfere with him when he chose to keep his capital to himself, and to make no use of it in trade, either by buying, or selling, or lending. Every "cheap-money" experiment that has ever been made has resulted in precisely the same demonstration, and the same fate awaits all those of the future.

CHAPTER IV

MODERN CHEAP – MONEY PANACEAS

IN the two chapters immediately preceding the present one we have set forth the details of two historical schemes for making money cheap and plentiful, that of the Land Bank in England in the latter part of the seventeenth century and that of the Paper Bank in Rhode Island at the close of the Revolutionary War. We intend now to consider some of the plans with similar purpose that are put forth by the leaders in various kinds of cheap-money movements which have gained headway in the Western States during the last year or more. With this consideration in view we have been making a collection of plans as they have been advanced from time to time in speeches and interviews. We append the more striking of these, giving the exact language in each instance, numbering them for convenience of reference but withholding the names of the originators in order that our subsequent remarks may be free from all appearance of personality.

1. I am not stuck on silver and gold as circulating me-
diums. A piece of paper is my ideal. Geologists have
things so fine that they can estimate the quantities of silver
and gold in the mountains, and the Government should
issue silver certificates to an amount equivalent to that
estimate. It would be far safer, as it would be easy for a
foreign nation to capture the coin in the treasury vaults at
Washington; but the mountains they could not remove,
even by all the faith they could muster.

2. People do not care whether a silver dollar contains
seventy cents' worth of silver or not, so long as it will buy
a dollar's worth of sugar or coffee. For fifteen of these
[holding up a copper cent] a man can buy copper enough to
make two dollars, yet it is good money.

3. We [speaking for the Farmers' Alliance] believe in the
people making their own money; we believe in the Government, which is simply the agent of the people, issuing their
money directly to them without going around Robin Hood's
barn to find them.

4. If the people had twice as much currency in their
pockets as now, their prosperity would be greatly increased.

5. I am in favor of more currency. We have n't enough
currency *per capita* to do the business of the country. If
we cannot increase the currency, I think somebody ought
to issue more collaterals. There is usually enough money
if a man has the collateral.

6. Under a free-coinage system I think people who have
small quantities of silver would be more apt to deal directly
with the Government, and the coin, flowing out of the mints
to them in smaller individual amounts, would quickly find
its way into the channels of ordinary trade. The rich speculators who now do most of the handling of the metal take
their big sums that they receive from the Government, and
use them in further speculation. Little enough of it ever
gets out in petty sums for circulation among the masses of '
the people.

7. My monetary system eliminates from money both the element of intrinsic value and the power to limit or control the value of things of use. I propose that the Government only shall issue money for the public use. In order to do this I would have it issue immediately 500,000,000 new treasury notes of the denomination of one dollar each. So much of this amount as was necessary the Government should loan to the people, ten per cent. of each loan to be paid back each year, nine per cent. to be applied to the extinction of the principal, and one per cent. covering the interest. In that way it would be possible to redeem every mortgaged farm in the land within fifteen years.

8. Banks should not be allowed to issue notes. These should be printed and put out by the Government. The tariff should be reduced till there is a deficit in the treasury, and then greenbacks should be printed and issued to pay all claimants. These should not be redeemable in metal money. Each bill should bear the legend: "One dollar, receivable for all dues and dbts." This would make it receivable for all taxes and import duties, and a legal tender. This would keep it perpetually at par.

9. Tens of thousands of our farmers have been unfortunate, and can never get out of debt without special relief. I would enact a law stopping the big interest they have agreed to pay, and substituting a debt at one per cent. interest. It would be done in this way. Suppose I owe you $5000 and accumulated interest on my farm. This new law would direct you to add the interest to the principal, and go to the treasury of my county and file the mortgage and an abstract of the property, and get a check on the nearest bank for the entire debt. That would satisfy you. Then the county treasurer makes a draft on the United States treasurer for the money, and gets it in crisp, new bills. That satisfies him. The United States treasurer accepts the mortgage on the farm, — providing it is worth the amount of the mortgage,— and sends word to me when the

one per cent. interest is due. Is not that simple? It is the first news I have had of the transfer of the debt. That ought to suit everybody.

These nine plans can be grouped into two general classes — those which preserve for the proposed cheap money some intrinsic value, and those which eliminate such value entirely. Of the former it is to be said that they are similar in character to the plans of the English Land Bank and the Rhode Island Paper Bank in that they propose the issue of money on land as security. The proposition for issuing notes against the estimated amount of silver and gold in a mountain is of course a proposition to issue them on the value of the land. They could be no more kept at par than the Rhode Island notes based on farm values could be, but would drop at once to a level of their own, which would inevitably be below the gold standard of value. As for the plans in the second group (those which favor paper money with nothing to fix its value save the Government stamp), they all contemplate a currency which the author of one of the plans (No. 8) says would be "perpetually at par"; that is to say, at par with itself. This was the peculiarity of the Continental, the Confederate, and the Rhode Island paper money, of the French assignats, and, in fact, of all inconvertible paper money ever issued. It is surely unnecessary, in view of unbroken human experience in testimony of the folly of such money, to

enter into a formal argument against it at this
late day. We shall continue to show its complete
failure in practice in subsequent articles upon experiments with it in various countries.

When we come to examine carefully these various plans we find that the advocates of all of them
are more or less perplexed as to the methods by
which the money, when it shall have been made
plenty by act of the Government, shall be got into
the "pockets of the people." This is the shoal
upon which many a fair cheap-money panacea has
been wrecked. The primal cause of every cheap-
money agitation is the same — a desire on the part
of people who are suffering from a scarcity of
money to possess more. They have nothing additional to offer in return for more,— that is, mer-
chandise, or goods, or labor, or product of any
kind,— but they imagine that the scarcity from
which they are suffering is due to the dearness of
the money itself, or to the financial policy of the
Government in limiting the amount issued, or to
some other cause than their own inability to raise
more, either by actual sale of something, or on
credit. When they are asked how they are going
to get possession of a share of the more plentiful
supply, and are held down to a specific answer,
their ingenuity is greatly taxed, and they turn to
their leaders for a solution of the difficulty. The
different ways in which the leaders, whose plans
we have collected, have met this demand furnish
most instructive material for study.

In the first and second plans this point is not touched upon. In the third the author says he favors issuing the money directly to the people, which seems to imply a free and unlimited distribution. In the fourth plan the incontrovertible assertion that "if the people had twice as much currency in their pockets as now, their prosperity would be greatly increased" is not accompanied with any suggestion as to how this doubling process can be accomplished. In the fifth — and this point we shall touch on later — the searching suggestion is dropped that perhaps an increase of collaterals is as much needed as an increase in currency. In the sixth the curious idea is brought forward that free coinage of silver would put money into the pockets of the people by enabling them to take what silver bullion they might happen to have on hand to the mints to be coined. In the seventh, eighth, and ninth plans an unlimited issue of inconvertible paper by the Government is advocated to be loaned to the people at one per cent., sometimes with land security and sometimes with none at all.

Of the relief which might come to the people by allowing them to have their own bullion coined, it is only to be said that it would depend entirely upon the amount of bullion which they had on hand and of the value of the silver dollars after they were coined. If the farmers of the West have bullion in considerable quantities stored about their premises, the fact is one which has not been suspected. Concerning the various plans for government loans of paper money at one per cent., the same comment can be made upon all of them. They would undoubtedly put money into the pockets of the people, but what would the money be worth? The farmers of Rhode Island had plenty of money put into their pockets in 1789, but they found that they could not buy anything with it save at heavy discount, could not use it in payment of mortgages and other debts, and that it paralyzed the commerce and industry of the State, and brought irreparable shame upon its honor. If the Government of the United States were to go into the business of lending money to the farmers in return for mortgage security, as some plans propose, or in return for no security, as others suggest, the only results would be that the entire farm mortgage debt of the country would be unloaded upon the Government, that farmers and all other people would have a lot of debased money in their pockets, and that in the end the credit of everybody, including that of the Government itself, would be undermined, if not completely destroyed.

The real need of the times is the one mentioned in the fifth plan; that is, for more collaterals. When the author of that plan says that "there is usually enough money if a man has the collateral," he shows that he has been a close and accurate observer. Collateral, as defined by "The Century Dictionary," is "anything of value, or representing

4

value, as bonds, deeds, etc., pledged as security in addition to a direct obligation." An advocate of cheap money was once going about Wall street complaining of the scarcity of money, and saying that all existing industrial, commercial, and financial woes came from a too small supply of currency. When he was told that there was plenty of money to be borrowed at low rates of interest, he retorted, "Ah, but that is only on first-class security." Money is always obtainable on that kind of security, and few people are ever to be found who wish to loan it on any other. The man who calls for more collaterals means to call for more first-class securities, for upon no others does any prudent man care to lend money. In other words, every man who has something of value to sell, or to lend, can get money of value in return. He can compel no man who has money to lend to lend it on any other than good security. As the value of the collateral goes down the rate of interest goes up, until it reaches the prohibitive point. If a loan which has been granted on condition of interest and principal being paid in sound or "dear" money be repaid, under legal authority, in "cheap" money, the inevitable effect is always to make it more difficult for any one to borrow on any except the most stringent terms thereafter; that is, on the best security, and with principal and interest payable in gold.

CHAPTER V

A NATION FOR A MORTGAGE

WE have in previous chapters set forth the details of two notable historical efforts to lighten the burdens of the people and to increase their wealth by making money cheap and plenty. In one the Land Bank experiment in England in 1696 was considered, and in another the Rhode Island Paper Bank experiment of 1786. We turned aside for a moment from the historical record to consider some of the modern cheap-money plans, in order to enforce upon our readers, while the English and the Rhode Island failures were fresh in their minds, the fact that these modern plans sought to repeat in our own times the disastrous experiments of one and two centuries ago. From that list of modern plans we purposely omitted one which may be said to have been the inspiring cause of nearly all those which we named. We refer to the Land Loan scheme of Senator Stanford of California. This, in brief, is that the Government shall lend an unlimited amount of money for twenty years at two per cent. interest

on land pledged as security at half its value; that
the value of the land shall be fixed by appraisers
appointed by a land-loan bureau in every county
in which a loan is applied for, their services to
be paid by the mortgagees; that there shall be
no limit to the amount of the money issued as
loans, except the needs of landowners, and their
ability to pledge the land; and that the bills
so issued shall be receivable for all taxes and all
debts.

This is in substance the Rhode Island experiment over again, but lest some one shall say that
that experiment was made in a State only, and
not in a nation, and hence had not the wealth of
the whole country to guarantee its success, we
shall not rely upon it as constituting a complete
demonstration of the fallacy of Mr. Stanford's
ideas. What was attempted in Rhode Island in
1786 was merely an imitation, on a small scale, of
what was done in France in 1718–20 under the
inspiration of the notorious adventurer and gam-
bler John Law. The history of his famous performances constitutes so perfect an answer to the
economists of Mr. Stanford's school that we shall
make it the subject of the present chapter in our
series.

John Law was the son of an Edinburgh jeweler
and money-changer. After a career of gambling,
dueling, and reckless adventure in every capital in
Europe, he turned his ingenuity to the invention
of schemes of finance and banking, and went about

from capital to capital seeking acceptance for them. Having had no success anywhere else, he appeared in Paris in 1716, just after the death of Louis XIV., when the regent, the Duke of Orleans, was confronted with a national debt of more than three billions, which made national bankruptcy imminent. He listened earnestly to Law when the latter assured him that the prosperity of a nation depended entirely upon the size of its circulating medium; that Holland with its wretched soil and dangerous shores was the richest country in the world simply because of its immense circulating medium; and that France by doubling its capital would enormously increase its wealth and resources, pay off its debts, and become the richest nation in the world. How could France double its capital? Why, easily enough. All it had to do was to establish a bank on the basis of all the actual property of the State.

A private bank which Law established succeeded very well, its bills being accepted by the Government. It really laid the foundation of credit in France, since it was the first bank of circulation and discount. Its success turned the heads of both Law and the regent. If with a small capital they could by means of credit circulate a volume of notes several times the size of the capital, what might they not do with the whole of France for capital? The private bank was dissolved in 1718, and the Government established the Royal Bank with Law as its director-general. He at once be-

gan to put into practice his idea of uniting all the
wealth of France into one great mass, and using
it as a basis upon which to issue an illimitable volume of notes. "He had conceived the idea," says
Blanqui, in his "History of Political Economy,"
"of combining into one common association all
the capitalists of France, and putting under their
control, as a loan, all the elements of public wealth
from landed property to the uncertain ventures of
colonial trade. What could be a finer mortgage
than France!"

As a part of his great "Company of the West,"
he included his famous Mississippi scheme. The
Chevalier La Salle, in his travels down the Mississippi River to the Gulf of Mexico, had taken
possession of all the territory through which it
flowed in the name of the French king, calling it,
in honor of Louis XIV., Louisiana. Law obtained
a concession of this district, gave dazzling accounts of its unlimited mineral and agricultural
wealth, and founded a commercial company upon
it with a capital of one hundred millions, divided
into two hundred thousand shares of five hundred
francs each. Other trading companies, the Ca-
nadian, Senegal, East Indian, and China, were also
taken into the bank and each made a "basis" for
the issue of notes. Then one after the other the
royal mint, the business of collecting the government taxes, and the receipts of the royal income
were included. Law's idea was to get all the receipts and all the issues of the nation into the

same hands, and then upon this vast basis, this
fine mortgage of France, to issue notes at will.

The shares of this company were eagerly
bought. He began the issue of paper money
guaranteed by the Government, and based upon
the value of all national property. " Bills issued
on land," he said, " are in effect coined land. Any
goods that have the qualities necessary in money
may be made money equal to their value. Five
ounces of gold is equal in value to £20, and may
be made money to that value; an acre of land is
equal to £20, and may be made money equal to
that value, for it has all the qualities necessary in
money." As a beginning, Law had notes to the
amount of one hundred and ten millions of pounds
sterling struck off and circulated. They were receivable in taxes, nominally redeemable in coin,
and made a legal tender. A great wave of instantaneous prosperity seemed to rush over France.
The parliament of Paris, alarmed by the furor
which seized the whole people, tried to check it
by legislation, but was overborne at once. Law
even threatened to abolish it for presuming to
stand in his way. The bank lent the king twelve
hundred billions of francs to pay off the debt.
An eye-witness of the scenes in Paris, writing at
the time, says: " All the town is in convulsion
over the shares; the capital is thrown into a kind
of state fever; we see the debt diminish before
our eyes; private fortunes are being made out of
nothing." From all parts of France men poured

into Paris to speculate. The street in which the bank was situated was crammed day and night. The shares rose to forty times their value in specie at the time of their issue. Everybody seemed to be getting richer, nobody poorer. The bank continued to pour forth paper money till its issue reached 3,071,000,000 francs, 833,000,000 more than it was legally authorized to emit. Its issue of shares at the extreme market value when the craze was at its height was twelve billion francs, which had been built up on an original issue of less than two millions.

M. Thiers, in his account of the situation at this time, says:

The variations of fortune were so rapid that stock-jobbers, receiving shares to sell, by keeping them one single day had time to make enormous profits. A story is told of one who, charged with selling some shares, did not appear for two days. It was thought the shares were stolen: not at all; he faithfully returned their value, but he had taken time to win a million for himself. This power which capital had of producing so rapidly had brought about a traffic; people lent the funds by the hour, and exacted unprecedented rates of interest. The stock-jobbers found, moreover, a way to pay the interest demanded and to reap a profit themselves. One could even gain a million a day.

Law himself reaped a colossal fortune in paper, which he turned into land as fast as he could. He bought no less than fourteen titled estates in France, a fact which is cited as evidence that he had faith in his own schemes, for had he been a swindler he would have invested his profits in some other country.

Of course such a condition of affairs could not last. Scarcely had the whole system been made complete before the inevitable collapse began to threaten. People began to sell their shares for land, houses, coin, or anything that had stable value. Prices rose enormously, and gold began to be hoarded. The shares began to fall and the paper money to depreciate. Then Law, like his imitators a half-century later in Rhode Island, began to try to save his paper money from destruction by edicts or forcing acts. It was forbidden to convert the notes into gold or silver, and decreed that they should bear a premium over specie. It was decreed that coin should be used only in small payments, and that only a small amount of it should be kept in the possession of private persons. Any one keeping more than 400 or 500 francs in specie was to be fined 10,000 francs. The wearing of gems and diamonds was prohibited. Nothing made of gold was to weigh over one ounce. Old specie was confiscated, and domiciliary visits were ordered to discover it. Of course these signs of desperation only hastened the end. The shares, which had been fluctuating wildly, began to go down steadily. This was in February, 1720, less than two years after the founding of the bank. When all the violent edicts failed to stop the decline, the Government decreed in May that the value of the shares and notes should be reduced one half. This was the end. The great bubble collapsed, for credit had been completely destroyed. The bank stopped payment, and the whole nation gave itself over to rage and despair. Law's life was in danger, and that of the regent was threatened. The bank was abolished; its notes were reconverted into the public debt, leaving it as it was when the bank was established; Law's estates were confiscated, and by November of 1720 not a trace of the bank or its various companies remained. Law himself remained in France till the end of the year, when he became a wanderer on the face of the earth, dying at Venice in 1729 almost a pauper. "Of all the industrial values produced under the hot atmosphere of Law's system," says Blanqui, "nothing remained but ruin, desolation, and bankruptcy. Landed property alone had not perished in the tempest."

This is the experiment which Senator Stanford proposes should be repeated in the United States. It is the same experiment which Rhode Island tried with similar results in 1786. It is the same experiment also which the Argentine Republic has been trying within the past five years, and the fruits which that unhappy country is now reaping from it we shall make the subject of our next chapter.

CHAPTER VI

THE ARGENTINE
CHEAP-MONEY PARADISE

IN many respects the experience through which the Argentine Republic is passing, in an attempt to increase the general prosperity by making money cheap and plentiful, comes closer to the American people than any of the similar efforts in other countries which have been described in previous chapters. The government of the Argentine Republic is closely modeled upon that of the United States. It is a country of almost boundless natural resources, whose development has been so rapid as to be almost without parallel in history, and whose growth in wealth, prosperity, and commercial importance has been so nearly approached by no other country in the world as by America. Its people are an energetic, buoyant, self-confident race, full of pride in their country and inclined to the belief that it is capable of withstanding any strain that may be put upon it. Yet, rich and prosperous as they were, these people conceived the idea, when a slight check to their development was felt a few years ago, that what they needed in order to attain the full measure of their prosperity was to make money "cheap and plenty." Perceiving the importance of their experience as an object-lesson for our own country, bearing as it does directly upon discussion and propositions current here, we have gone thoroughly into the matter, examining all available sources of information, and have thus been able to prepare for our readers what we believe to be the most complete as well as accurate account yet published.

In 1873 there was established in the capital city of the Argentine Republic, Buenos Ayres, the Hypothecary or Mortgage Bank, whose main object was to make loans on all kinds of landed property. The principles upon which these loans were to be made were much the same as Senator Stanford is advocating as a basis for similar loans by the United States Government. Any person owning landed property in the province could go to the bank and secure a loan for half its value, which was to be fixed by the bank's appraisers. The bank gave him a mortgage-bond, called a cédula, which was to run for twenty-four years, at from six to eight per cent. interest, two per cent. amortization, and one per cent. commission. The interest was payable quarterly, and there were coupons attached for the twenty-four years. The cédulas were issued in alphabetical series, beginning with A and running to P. They were bought and sold on the Bolsa or Stock-exchange, and from their first issue became an important element in speculation. The first issue of series A was between $13,000,000 and $14,000,000, the Argentine dollar being about ninety-six cents of our money, being based upon the unit of the French monetary system. These remained at par for only a short time after issue. They were quickly followed by others, until series A closed with a total issue of $27,394,-000. Then came series B with an issue of $1,092,-000, series C with $813,000, series D with $288,000, all at seven per cent. Then came series E with a total issue of $15,830,000 at six per cent., and F with a total issue of $6,100,000 at seven per cent. Ten years after the bank's establishment over $100,-000,000 of these cédulas had been issued, all based, be it remembered, upon the landed property of a single province. They had from the outset been used for speculative purposes, and every year this use became more wild and reckless. A ring was formed between directors of the bank and certain favored brokers for the absolute control of the successive issues. No one could obtain concession for a loan who did not make application through these brokers, and in order that all the members of the ring might reap their share of the profit, the value of the property upon which the loans were placed was raised to extravagant figures.

The fictitious prosperity which the Hypothecary Bank brought to Buenos Ayres infected the entire republic, and in 1884 Congress passed a law an-

5

nexing a National Hypothecary Bank to the National Bank, which was the fiscal agent of the Government and of all the provinces except Buenos Ayres. The issue of cédulas on the landed property of the nation was authorized, for fifty per cent. of its value, at interest from six to eight per cent., with two per cent. amortization and one per cent. commission, no single loan to exceed $250,000, and all payable at the end of twelve years. The issue of cédulas was at first limited to $40,000,000, but this was extended from time to time so that in November, 1890, six years after the National Bank began the experiment, it had out no less than $204,000,000 in gold, all bearing interest. The Buenos Ayres Bank had increased its issue of cédulas so that at the same date it had no less than $330,000,000, but these were in paper, making the grand total of money which had been loaned upon land in the republic during seventeen years $534,000,000, or $140 for every man, woman, and child.

When the National Bank went into the hypothecary business in 1884 paper money was at par with gold. Several severe checks to the national prosperity were felt during that year. Cholera made necessary a rigorous quarantine against Mediterranean steamers and checked immigration. Heavy floods during the fall delayed the shipment of crops from the interior to the seaboard. A new Government loan of $90,000,000 was to be placed; but the European market, which was expected to

take $10,000,000 of it, was so nearly sated with
Argentine investments of one kind or another
that it declined to take more than $3,500,000.

In January, 1885, a run began upon the Provincial Bank of Buenos Ayres, and compelled it to
suspend specie payments; whereupon the President of the republic declared the national currency
a legal tender. Gold rose at once to 17 per cent.
premium, and then to 20 per cent. In February
it had reached 33 per cent., and it continued to rise
steadily till at one time it was at 350 per cent.;
that is to say, $450 in paper was worth only $100
in gold. From the moment that the gold standard was abandoned, the demand for more paper
money began to be heard, and it was poured out
by the Government in almost unlimited volume.
Under the pretense of creating a sounder financial
system and securing a more stable currency, a law
was passed in November, 1887, establishing a system of State Banks, forty in number, similar to
our National Banks. These started with a capital
of $350,000,000, and began to issue paper money,
not being required, as our banks are, to be able at
all times to redeem their notes with gold.

When the premium on gold had reached 40
per cent., the Government took the position that
the increase was a trick of the brokers, and
not in any way an outcome of currency inflation, and issued a decree allowing the banks to
issue currency practically without limit. At the
same time the Government, to satisfy the de-

mand for gold, and to prove its belief in its own contentions, threw $30,000,000 of its gold reserves on the market. The gold premium continued to rise with no perceptible check, and as it rose the banks poured out more and more paper money in a frenzied attempt to check its upward flight.

It was discovered after a time that, through trickery, there were several millions more of this irredeemable paper money in circulation than had been supposed. A provision of the national banking law required that all banks reorganizing under it should withdraw and cancel their old notes when they put their new ones in circulation. Several banks, in collusion with dishonest officials, violated this requirement, and kept a large part of their old issue in circulation with the new. At one time the amount of this fraudulent money, based on nothing whatever, amounted to $60,000,-000. Some of this was afterward destroyed, but the latest official estimate put the amount still in circulation at over $35,000,000. As the latest attainable total of the regular paper issue of the banks places it at $345,000,000, the grand total of paper money in circulation in March of last year, worth about 25 cents on a dollar, was $380,000,-000, all irredeemable, and decreasing in value every day. This was a *per capita* circulation of $100 for every man, woman, and child in the republic. That ought certainly to have put "plenty of money in the pockets of the people," for $100 is the highest sum *per capita* our wildest cheap-money advocates have ever demanded.

With the entry of the National Bank into the business of loaning money on land, the whole country plunged into a wild debauch of speculation, which closely resembled that through which France passed when the same financial experiment was made under John Law's inspiration, as described in the preceding chapter. All kinds of property acquired a fictitious value, and were made the basis for loans at that valuation. The Government, departing with complete abandon from all the limitations of legitimate government, helped on the popular furor by giving its aid and sanction to all kinds of mushroom banking, building, and colonization enterprises designed to "boom" the value of property and increase its loanable capacity. The country was sprinkled all over with banks pouring out millions of paper money which could never be redeemed, and thickly studded with inflated joint-stock companies with millions of capital on paper, whose business it was to get from the banks loans for many times the real value of the property upon which they were based. When the banks had exhausted all their capital in loans, the Government, assuming their indebtedness, gave them millions of gold with which to continue the issue of cédulas. The business of speculating in gold became enormously profitable, and private banks made fortunes. Men made 10 per cent. per week in the business, and 20 to 24 per cent. per annum was the usual profit. A Bank of Construction was conceived and put in operation by an unscrupulous speculator, which, in collusion with dishonest Government officials, bought vast amounts of property, improved it, obtained exaggerated loans upon it, and sold it in such dishonest ways that the interest on the loans could never be collected. The speculator made a colossal fortune; the stock of his bank went to enormous figures on the Bolsa, but, when the tide turned, fell 100 points in a single day, carrying ruin to hundreds of men who fancied themselves rich.

Many of the early cédulas had been sent abroad, and their ready sale in London, Paris, and Berlin had encouraged their further issue. About $15,-000,000 in all were taken abroad, and more would have been bought had not the European market been flooded with Argentine loans between 1881 and 1890. These were instituted or backed by the Argentine government, and consisted chiefly of loans either to the Government or to provinces or to cities. They were for nearly every conceivable purpose — railways, harbors, street-paving, public buildings, school-houses, markets, tenement-houses, bridges, theaters, hospitals, boulevards, public squares, and drainage. In December, 1889, the aggregate of these loans, taken largely in England, was over $122,000,000 for the republic and over $193,500,000 for the provinces, and the total amount of gold which had to be exported annually from the Argentine Republic to pay the interest on its foreign indebtedness, and dividends on railway, bank, and other stocks held abroad, was over $75,000,000. With a foreign debt of $315,500,000, there had been accumulated at the close of 1889 an internal national debt of $207,000,000, and an internal provincial debt of $44,000,000, making at the close of that year a grand total debt of $566,500,000. This has since been increased to $772,500,000. As the population of the republic is about 3,800,000, the debt is over $203 for every inhabitant.

It is small wonder that under this mountain of debt the National Government is bankrupt, having neither money nor credit, and that it anticipates a deficit for the current year of over $17,000,000. The provincial deficit for the current year is estimated at between $4,000,000 and $5,000,000, making a probable deficit in the whole republic of nearly or quite $22,000,000.

Affairs have been going from bad to worse since the crisis of 1890. Credit practically collapsed in the spring of that year. After that time the provincial banks were not able to meet their obligations. The lands upon which loans were based became unsalable, cédulas dropped to 50 and even 35 cents on the dollar, which was equivalent to 13 and 9 cents respectively in gold. The paper dollar was worth about 25 cents. The Provincial Bank of Buenos Ayres, which was the savings-bank of the working-classes, stopped paying its obligations in 1890, and the National Bank passed its dividend. A revolution broke out, and though the Government quelled it the President was forced to resign.

Investigations instituted by the new government into the condition of the banks revealed astounding rottenness and corruption. The whole power of the Government was exerted for several months to prevent the National Bank and the Provincial Bank of Buenos Ayres from being publicly declared insolvent, but on April 8, 1891, the President gave up the struggle and issued a formal decree for the liquidation of both, all payments being suspended till June 1. The time was subsequently extended twenty days by Congress, and then extended indefinitely.

This was the end, and the wreck of the banks was complete. In 1886 the National Bank had a capital of £10,000,000 sterling, and the Provincial Bank one of £8,000,000 sterling. Not a penny of the latter remained. The National Bank had lost £8,800,000 of its £10,000,000, and owed the Government £14,000,000. These two banks had lost, therefore, during five years' experience with cheap money based on landed property, about £30,000,000 sterling, a sum more than double the capital of the Bank of England.

When the collapse came the nation gave itself over, as France had done two centuries earlier, to rage and despair. Men who were believed to be worth millions found themselves paupers. One man who had been worth $20,000,000, which he had accumulated during a lifetime's devotion to honest industry, but who had been tempted to venture it in speculation, lost every dollar. He had just completed the building of a house of palatial magnificence, costing $180,000, but had never entered it, when the crisis came, and it was taken to pay his debts. A United States minister to a South American government, who was in Buenos Ayres at the time, thus describes the condition of the nation:

In six months the people have passed from commercial activity and enthusiasm to depression; from happiness to misery; from confidence to despair. They have taken a Niagara plunge, from which they will not recover in a generation. The worst of the scheme was that it offered irresistible temptation to bribery. It made it possible for any man who owned real estate to get almost any quantity of money, if he would only swear falsely. An acquaintance of mine had a nice farm there which he valued at $15,000. The law would give him a loan to one half of the value—that value to be fixed by the official appraisers. He "saw" the appraisers, and he obtained a loan of Government money —cédula—amounting to $250,000, the maximum loan permitted by law to one person. Think of it! And the money was indorsed by the Barings, the great London bankers! Of course the appraisers got half of it, but the people have it to pay. And they are now in debt more than $100 for every man, woman, and child—hopelessly bankrupt.

Mr. E. L. Baker, the United States consul at Buenos Ayres, to whose valuable reports we are indebted for much of the information contained in this chapter, says under date of November 17, 1890:

The collapse has come, and come with a vengeance. Lands unsalable at any price; national banks gutted and left without a cent in their strong boxes; stock companies with fraudulent entries in their records and without anything to show for the pretensions they set up; merchants unable to meet their liabilities in bank; notes protested and extensions granted; the general business at a standstill; the banks hesitating to discount; and nobody able to say whom it is safe to trust — such is the picture which the country presents to-day. . . . Every business, every industry, every new enterprise feels and suffers from the tremendous reaction which has taken place. Everybody is confounded and stands aghast, looking at the stick which but yesterday, as it were, was a flaming rocket. . . . The truth is the Argentine Republic is suffering from a paralysis of credit. . . . The "fool's paradise" in which the Argentine people have been living for the last few years must be wiped out of existence. Inflation must give place to "hard pan." . . . It has been the general boast among those who were pushing on the "boom" that this was an "exceptional country," and that the ordinary laws of trade, currency, and banking, however requisite to be followed in such countries as England or the United States, had no significance or applicability in the Argentine Republic. Here, it was insisted, all manner of violations of economic principles could be practised with impunity, and the country would flourish by the outrage. The present prostrate condition of both public and private credit shows the inherent fallacy of such an assumption. I only fear that the country will for a long time have to walk in the valley of humiliation and endure a protracted period of business and financial depression before it will again be able to hold up its head and present that buoyant and triumphant look which it has heretofore so proudly worn.

This is the experiment which men imbued with Senator Stanford's ideas are seeking to have the United States undertake. They are advocating it with precisely the same kind of talk which Mr. Baker quotes as having been heard in the Argentine Republic. They are calling the United States an "exceptional country" which is so great and prosperous that it can defy not merely economic laws, but the teaching of all human experience. The consequences of the Argentine experiment were felt not only in that republic, but they convulsed the financial centers of three great European countries and virtually ruined the first banking house of England. The effect was so severely felt in this country that a panic was imminent nearly every day for several weeks, while all branches of trade suffered a mysterious and numbing paralysis.

In the gain or loss of one race all the rest have equal claim,

says Lowell, and of nothing is this more true than of the observance by a nation of the great laws of common honesty and fair dealing which lie at the foundation of all economic science.

CHAPTER VII

THE SUBTREASURY
CHEAP-MONEY PLAN

THE subtreasury scheme of the Farmers' Alliance is in many respects the most extreme form in which the cheap-money delusion in this country has manifested itself. It is so extreme, in fact, that many of the Alliance leaders have refused from the outset to give it their approval, and others of them who at first viewed it with favor, after examination and discussion of its provisions have withdrawn their approval. At first it made great headway in the South, but earnest, intelligent, and courageous exposure of its dangerous fallacies by leading politicians and newspapers has so far educated the people upon the economic principles involved that it has been losing ground perceptibly during the past year. A veritable campaign of education has been made in several Southern States, with this scheme as the text of public discussion, and the beneficial results afford a striking illustration of the high patriotic service of courage and conviction in politics and journalism.

The subtreasury scheme made its appearance in the Fifty-first Congress, when a bill embodying its principles was introduced in both houses, having been prepared by the National Legislative Committee of the Farmers' Alliance. Briefly summed up, it provided for the appropriation by the Government of $50,000,000 to be used for the erection of warehouses in various parts of the country for the storage of cotton, wheat, oats, corn, and tobacco. Every county which had an annual production of these staples exceeding $500,000 in gross value was to be entitled to a warehouse. A petition was to be sent to the Secretary of the Treasury asking for its establishment, accompanied by the title of a suitable site to be given to the Government. The Secretary of the Treasury was to appoint a manager, who should give bonds for the faithful performance of his duties, and should receive a salary of not less than $1000 and of not more than $2500, proportionate to the business done. Any owner of cotton, wheat, corn, oats, or tobacco might take his crop to the nearest warehouse, deposit it, and receive in return eighty per cent. of its market value in treasury notes, the manager deciding what that market value should be. These treasury notes were to be specially issued for this purpose by the Secretary, no note to be less than $1 nor more than $1000, to be legal tender for all public and private debts, and good as part of the lawful reserve of national banks. The manager was to give a receipt for every deposit of produce, show-

6

ing its amount, grade, or quality, value at date of deposit, and amount advanced upon it, with rate of interest one per cent. per annum, and with insurance, weighing, warehousing, classing, and other charges deducted. These receipts were to be negotiable by indorsement. Produce deposited might be redeemed at any time by a return of the receipt and money advanced on interest, and the payment of all warehousing charges. The money returned was to be destroyed by the Secretary of the Treasury. If there were no redemption of a deposit within twelve months, a sale was to be ordered for the reimbursement of the Government.

Let us see how this would work in practice. The warehouse managers, who are to decide upon the market price of the produce, would, in nearly all instances, be appointed through political influence, which is tantamount to saying that they would have little expert knowledge of the duties which they were to perform. These men would have absolute power to decide upon the sums of which the Government was to advance eighty per cent. There are, for example, eleven full grades of cotton, and about as many half grades, and there are about thirty grades of wheat. The manager must decide not merely the grade, but the price as it is fixed in the markets of the world at the time. If he were an honest man and fairly capable, the opportunity for serious blunders would be very great. If he were a dishonest, or ignorant, or prejudiced, or malicious man, can any one estimate the evil and injustice of which he might be capable? He could overrate the produce of all his political and personal friends, and underrate that of all his enemies or rivals, and there would be no appeal from his decisions. The impossibility of having a just and uniform basis for the eighty per cent. advance in all the warehouses, or even in one of them, would from the outset throw fatal doubt upon the value both of the treasury notes and of the certificates of deposit, giving them at once a depreciated and uncertain standard.

The farmers who are misled into favoring the scheme think that they would receive at once a loan of eighty per cent. of the full value of their crop at only one per cent. interest, but they would pay much more than that. The warehousing, insurance, and other expenses for cotton, for example, are usually between eight and nine per cent. of its value. This would have to be paid to the Government, and would bring the interest up to nine or ten per cent. On wheat and other products there would be similar expenses, which would raise the interest on deposits of them to nearly or quite the same limits. The rate of interest, therefore, is not low enough to be beneficial to farmers who hope by this means to pay off existing debts at legal rates of interest. What a farmer would receive would be a loan for one year from the Government, at the rate of nine or ten per cent., of a sum amounting to four fifths of the total value of his crop, paid to him in money of uncertain value.

For the remaining fifth he would receive a certificate whose value would depend entirely upon what he got for it in open market. No buyer would ever offer him the full price as fixed by the warehouse manager, for there would be too many uncertainties about the crop's redemption to make the certificate a safe investment for anybody. They could be negotiated only at a heavy discount at best, and in many instances would scarcely be negotiable at all.

If warehouses were established, there would be a tendency among all farmers seeking an immediate market to put their produce into them. One of the advocates of the scheme estimated before a committee of the Senate that the deposits would be so large as to require an addition of one thousand millions of dollars to the currency in January and February of each year. This flood of currency, all of which would be based upon the uncertain and varying bases of valuation, would be accompanied by another flood of certificates of deposit. The Government would turn out these notes and certificates, and their receivers would at once put them in circulation. Their value would depend entirely upon the popular estimate which should be made of their purchasing power. The fact that the notes had been declared a legal tender would not add a particle to their value. The people would make their own estimate of the prospect for the fulfilment of the promise upon which they were based, and that estimate would fix their value.

What would be the prospect for this promise to be fully kept? If prices went down after the deposit, the produce would be left there till the very end of the year and sold for what it would bring. The effect of throwing a great mass of produce upon the market at one time would be to lower still further the price, and the result would be a great loss to the Government, which must be made good by taxation. As the farmers of the country pay about half of the taxes, they would thus have to pay half of the cost of their own folly. From the nature of the case a falling off in value would be almost inevitable, for speculators and purchasers would be interested in waiting for a forced sale, being thus certain of buying at a lower price. In case there should be a general rise after deposit, the chances would be that the farmers most in need of profiting by it would not be in a position to do so, for the poorer ones would have parted with their notes as soon as received, in payment of their debts, and would have also sold their deposit certificates at the first opportunity. Whatever rise there might be, therefore, would go to the advantage of the speculators in certificates.

As for the depreciated value of the notes issued in such volume, there can be no doubt upon that point. It would be fiat money of a more worthless kind than any which has hitherto been issued. It would be more worthless than the Land Bank money of Rhode Island, because that was based upon the land of the State. It would be more worthless than that of John Law's bank in France, for that was based upon all the property of France. It would be more worthless than that of the Argentine Republic, for that was based upon all the landed property of the nation. In all these instances the fiat money was declared to be a legal tender and to be payable for public and private debts. In all of them it was issued for a term of years. But this warehouse-deposit money is based upon nothing except the arbitrary judgments of an irresponsible body of political appointees as to the value of products a year hence, and is to be destroyed at the end of a year. Nobody would ever consent to take it at its face-value in payment of a debt, or in payment for goods, and it would be confined, as the Rhode Island paper money was, almost entirely to transactions among its original holders. It would enormously inflate prices in the communities in which it circulated, and thus make dearer everything that the farmer had to buy. But it would never be received elsewhere except at a discount, and consequently would have no effect in raising the price of the products of the farmer, which have to be sold in the markets of the world. Then, too, each period of enormous inflation would be followed by a period of sudden and almost paralyzing contraction, for at the end of each year all the notes and certificates must be destroyed.

We have said nothing about the unconstitutional aspect of the proposition for the Government to go into the business of loaning money and speculating in crops—a form of paternalism the most extreme ever proposed in this country. One of the advocates of the measure, when asked at a hearing before a Congressional committee why its authors had not included wool, hops, rice, and cheese with the other produce specified for deposit, made answer that those staples were protected by a high tariff, 75 per cent. on wool alone, and were not entitled to further aid from the Government. Whatever virtues may reside in the protective system, it is unfortunately true that to the arguments advanced in defense of a high tariff we owe the impression, so strong among many portions of the population, that it is the duty of the Government to render assistance to all industries and occupations whose members are in distress.

CHAPTER VIII

THE "PER CAPITA" DELUSION

THE *per capita* argument has always been a favorite method for sustaining a demand for cheap money. Such demands invariably arise when times are hard; that is, when money is scarce. The cheap-money advocates, acting on the knowledge that a great many people are wishing that they had more money in their pockets, come forward with the explanation that the real cause of the trouble is the smallness of the monetary circulation, the volume of currency not being adequate for the demands of the business of the country. They point to other countries, like England, Germany, and France, saying that they have a much larger *per capita* circulation than the United States, and claim that everybody in this country would have more money in his pocket if a great addition of some form of cheap money—either irredeemable paper, or depreciated silver, or subtreasury notes—were made to the currency.

The fundamental defect in the argument is that it confounds small circulation with small distribution. The trouble is not that the circulation is small, but that so many people fail to get much of it. If the circulation were to be doubled, or trebled, or quadrupled, what reason is there for believing that the people who have least at present would have any more? *How would they go to work to get some of the increase into their pockets?* This, as we said in one of the earlier chapters, is the crucial question in all schemes for making money cheap and plentiful. How can a man who wants some of it obtain it except he give labor or goods in return for it? If he have labor or goods to sell, does it make any difference to him whether the volume of currency be large or small? Is it not always large enough to furnish payment for what he has to sell? And if he has anything to sell, would not he rather receive his payment in dear money than in cheap money? Was there ever a man yet who did not desire to be paid for his wares in the soundest and best money obtainable? Who are the men who hope, in some mysterious manner, to get money into their pockets through a great issue of cheap money by the Government? Are they not, almost invariably, men who have nothing to sell in exchange for it?

It is difficult to see why the *per capita* argument should influence any one who thinks about it carefully. When we say that the wealth of the country if divided equally among all its inhabitants would be so many dollars *per capita*, nobody is seriously disturbed by the fact. Nobody says

that there is not wealth enough in the country.
The most usual observation is that it is a pity it
cannot be more evenly distributed. But when the
statement is made that the circulation is only $23
per capita, many people are inclined to think that
this is not enough, and that if we had more everybody would be in more comfortable circumstances.
But would everybody get some of the increase
into his pocket? If not, what would be the advantage? If the wealth of the country were to
be doubled, where would the increase go? The
greater part of it would go to the millionaires and
other rich people who have most at present, while
the people who have least would get little or none
of it. So it would be with an increase of circulating medium. If the *per capita* were to be doubled,
the ratio of the present division would be maintained. The people who had the most before
would get the most of the increase, while those
who had none before would get none now. The
great want of the people who have none is not an
increase in the volume of currency, but the dis-
covery of a new method by which they can get
some of the currency already in circulation into
their pockets.

Statistics published lately by the Treasury De-
partment demonstrate conclusively the fallacy of
the *per capita* argument. These give the *per
capita* circulation for each year from 1860 down
to the present time, and show that there has been
a steady rise from $17.50 in 1870 to $23.45 in 1891.

If prosperity is determined by *per capita*, this country ought to be vastly better off in 1890–1891 than it was in 1870, but, as a matter of fact, 1870 was one of the most prosperous years the country has ever known, while 1890 and 1891 will be known in history as years of almost unequaled financial and industrial depression. All through the years since 1878 we have been swelling the volume of currency by coining silver and gold to the amount of $945,000,000, and have been issuing many millions more of silver notes and gold notes, till we have now a circulation of over $1,500,000,000 against only a little more than $655,000,000 in 1870.

Those persons who were complaining a few months ago, when money was scarce, that even this immense volume of currency was insufficient for the business needs of the country, and that if we had a larger circulation *per capita* there would be no such scarcity, were laboring under a misapprehension. They were confounding contraction of the currency with contraction of credit. Ninety-two per cent. of all the business of the country is done on credit, and only eight per cent. with actual currency. When, therefore, credit is unsettled as it was by the impending peril of free-silver coinage, which would have lowered the standard of value as well as destroyed its stability, instantly a serious monetary contraction was felt throughout all the avenues of trade. Instead of the trouble being one which an issue of cheap money would

have remedied, it was one which owed its existence
entirely to the mere threat of such issue. As soon
as the threatened danger was averted, the strin-
gency disappeared, and there has been no complaint heard since about a scarcity of money,
either for "moving the crops" or for anything
else.

Suppose now that free coinage of silver were
to be authorized, what would be the effect upon
the circulation? It is estimated that $12,000,000
would be the extreme amount that it could add to
the circulation. If the increase of nearly a billion
since 1870 has not helped us, would twelve millions
do it? And if we were to have free coinage, into
whose pockets would the increase go? Not into
those of the people, but into those of the men
who sold the silver to the Government at a price
greater than it would be worth as money after
being coined. Those men would not put it into
the pockets of the people, but would add it to
their own wealth, and the only benefit the people
would derive would be the opportunity to pay off
their debts in a cheaper money than that in which
they were incurred, provided they were able to
get some of it in return for labor or goods.

Per capita arguments from foreign countries
are all misleading. Nobody can tell what the *per
capita* circulation of Germany, France, and England is, because those countries have a metallic
circulation of large and unknown volume, with
no small bank-notes like ours. The systems in

all these countries are so different from ours that
intelligible comparison is out of the question.

If size of *per capita* circulation determines prosperity, how does it happen that the Argentine
Republic, with a *per capita* of over one hundred
dollars, is in such financial, commercial, and industrial collapse? How did it happen that repeated additions to its volume of currency did
not check its downward march to ruin?

The delusion behind the *per capita* argument is
the same one that is behind all cheap-money panaceas. It is a belief, not always clearly defined,
that a large issue of money by the Government
will carry with it in some mysterious way an instru-
mentality for getting some of that money into the
pockets of the people without the people giving
anything in return for it. It is based on the idea
that the Government can *create* money, and is a perfectly logical deduction from that idea, for if the
Government can create money, there is no reason
why it should not distribute it freely among the people. In fact, if the Government can create money,
and by its own edict maintain it in circulation as
good as any other money, *why should the Government
levy taxes?* This question has been asked before,
but we have never seen or heard an answer to it.
If the Government can take 75 cents' worth of
silver, and by declaring it to be a dollar make it
worth 100 cents, why should it not do the same
with 50 cents' worth, or 10 cents' worth, or with a
piece of paper? And having done this, having

7

by its fiat made a piece of paper worth a dollar, why, we ask again, should it not abolish taxation and support itself with the money of its own creation? If it were to do that it would give us a *per capita* circulation greater than any the world has yet seen.

CHAPTER IX

MICHIGAN'S "WILD-CAT" BANKS

THE history of Michigan's "wild-cat" banking experience, while not so applicable to present financial discussion as other cheap-money experiments which we have cited in previous chapters, is nevertheless instructive for two reasons: first, because it was an attempt to make "hard times" easier by unlimited issues of irredeemable paper money, and second, because the money so issued was based largely on land as security. For these reasons it has seemed to us worth while to recall it at the present time.

Michigan became a State in January, 1837. Almost the first act of her State legislature was the passage of a general banking law under which any ten or more freeholders of any county might organize themselves into a corporation for the transaction of banking business. Of the nominal capital of a bank only ten per cent. in specie was required to be paid when subscriptions to the stock were made, and twenty per cent. additional in specie when the bank began business. For the further security of the notes which were to be issued as currency, the stockholders were to give first mortgages upon real estate, to be estimated at its cash value by at least three county officers, the mortgages to be filed with the auditor-general of the State. A bank commissioner was appointed to superintend the organization of the banks, and to attest the legality of their proceedings to the auditor-general, who, upon receiving such attestation, was to deliver to the banks circulating notes amounting to two and a half times the capital certified to as having been paid in.

This law was passed in obedience to a popular cry that the banking business had become an "odious monopoly" that ought to be broken up. Its design was to "introduce free competition into what was considered a profitable branch of business heretofore monopolized by a few favored corporations." Anybody was to be given fair opportunities for entering the business on equal terms with everybody else. The act was passed in March, 1837, and the legislature adjourned till November 9 following. Before the latter date arrived, in fact before any banks had been organized under the law, a financial panic seized the whole country. An era of wild speculation reached a climax, the banks in all the principal cities of the country suspended specie payments, and State legislatures were called together to devise remedies to meet the situation. That of Michigan was convened in special session in June, and its remedy for the case of Michigan was to leave the general banking law in force, and to add to it full authority for banks organized under it to begin the business of issuing bills in a state of suspension—that is, to flood the State with an irredeemable currency, based upon thirty per cent. of specie and seventy per cent. of land mortgage bonds. The law was so modified that any number of persons, upon signing an agreement to that effect, might become a banking corporation, and almost any one might become a director.

Everybody in the State who was in debt, and everybody who saw in the law an opportunity for rascality, went into the banking business. Within a few months wherever two roads crossed a bank was established. One was found in a sawmill, and one of the official records of the period says: "Every village plot with a house, or even without a house, if it had a hollow stump to serve as a vault, was the site of a bank." Many of them had no offices, no books, and no capital. Judge T. M. Cooley, in an interesting account of the experience in his history of Michigan, published in the "American Commonwealths" series, says (p. 267): "Wild lands that had been recently bought of the government at one dollar and twenty-five cents an acre were now valued at ten or twenty times that amount, and lots in villages that still existed only on paper had a worth for banking purposes only limited by the conscience of the officer who was to take the securities."

As for the requirements for ten per cent. payment in specie at the time of subscription, and twenty per cent. before beginning banking business, these were soon got around in ways more unscrupulous than ingenious. As the payments were to be made to the banks themselves, the same specie could be used many times over. Sometimes a small sum in specie was paid in and taken out, and the process repeated over and over, till the amount required was made to appear as having been received. Sometimes specie certificates, stating that the maker held a sum of specie for the bank, were counted as specie. These were almost invariably false, and they were made to do service for many banks in succession. If specie was actually used, as soon as the bank examiner had seen it it was hurried into a wagon and taken with fleet horses to another bank, where it again did duty as capital. "Gold and silver," say the official chroniclers, "flew about the country like magic; its sound was heard in the depths of the forest, yet, like the wind, one knew not whence it came or whither it was going." Sometimes what seemed to the eye of the examiner to be kegs of specie were really kegs of nails or window-glass with a thin layer of coin on top. The loan of specie to be used in the establishing of banks became a regular and lucrative branch of banking business.

Within one year forty-nine banks were organized, and forty went into operation with a professed capital of $1,745,000, of which thirty per cent. was claimed to have been paid in in specie. Over $2,000,000 of irredeemable paper was distributed throughout the State, of which probably not a dollar was based on *bona fide* capital paid in for legitimate banking purposes. As was inevitable, there was no public confidence in money of this character. Whoever received it got rid of it as soon as possible. It was always at a great discount with the money of Eastern banks, and some of it was rated much higher than the rest. Much of it was never circulated near the places of issue, which were selected often in spots as inaccessible as possible, in order that the bills might not soon return to plague their sponsors. Adventurers from New York and other distant places went into the wilds of the State, located banks, took the entire issue of money, and put it in circulation anywhere but near the place of issue.

The commissioners used all possible vigilance to close up bogus banks, but as fast as they closed them others were started. When a "wild-cat" bank either failed or was put in the hands of a receiver the farmers and laboring people suffered the most severely, as is always the case in such disasters. The plague ran its course in about a year and a half. At the end of 1839 there were no fewer than forty-two "wild-cat" banks in the hands of receivers, and only four still doing business. Nearly all the currency of the State was worthless, business was prostrate, values of all kinds had been nearly or quite destroyed. There was no buying or selling of land, and only the bare necessities of life were able to command a market.

The banking law was taken before the courts and declared unconstitutional, and the system was abolished, leaving behind it no assets, but boundless ruin.

In summing up the results, Judge Cooley, in language which many modern advocates of cheap money may peruse with profit, says: "Such were the fruits of the experiment of giving equal and practically unlimited rights in banking to everybody who wanted a shorter road to wealth than that trodden by labor and honest industry. The new State, under the bold but inexperienced guidance of its youthful governor, disdaining the lessons of history, had determined to try for itself the experiment of manufacturing money by the printing-press. The condition after the experiment might be compared to a forest after a cyclone; everything was prostrate, and everything was in confusion! . . . Thereafter wild-cat banking was a byword in the State; but the lessons it taught needed to be learned at some time, and were not likely to be learned except with experience as a teacher. One of its lessons was that neither real estate nor anything else not immediately convertible into money can support the credit of bank currency." This lesson is as applicable to the whole country as it was to Michigan, for even the United States Government is not powerful enough to support the credit of bank currency in real estate or anything else not immediately convertible into money.   This is, more- . over, the lesson of all human experience.

CHAPTER X

ALABAMA'S THOUSAND-DOLLAR-A-DAY BLUNDER

ALABAMA'S experience with banking "in the interests of the people" was in some respects similar to that of Michigan with " wild-cat " banks. Like that of many other States at about the same period, it resulted in complete collapse, with great financial loss to the people whom it was designed to benefit, a serious impairment of the State's credit, a flood of public scandal, and a heavy burden of debt. The history of Alabama's blunder is so full of instruction for those who believe in State or national agency for making everybody prosperous by means of liberal banking and cheap money, that we shall set it forth in some detail.

Alabama went into the banking business as a State in 1823, when its legislature passed an act for the establishment of the Bank of the State of Alabama, the capital, which was not limited to any amount, to be furnished entirely by the State. The management of the bank was intrusted to a president and twelve directors, who were to be

chosen annually by joint vote of the legislature.
The only limit put to the volume of notes which
the bank should issue was that they should be in
such sums as the president and directors might
deem "most expedient and safe." Certain public
funds were set aside to constitute part of the capital of the bank, and in addition the State was
authorized to issue State stock to the amount of
$100,000, redeemable within ten years, and bearing
interest not exceeding 6 per cent. The bank began
business in 1825. Three years later it was authorized to issue $100,000 more of State stock, redeem-
able in twenty years, at a rate of interest not exceeding 6 per cent. In the same year other public
funds, aggregating $1,300,000, were added to the
capital. Five years later about $500,000 of State
University funds were transferred to the bank as
capital. Between 1832 and 1835 four branches of
the State Bank were established in as many cities,
and State bonds to the amount of $6,300,000 were
issued to supply them with capital.

The design of the founders of the system was to
distribute the bank money as evenly as possible
among the people of the State, and with this end
in view the original act stipulated that the money
loaned by the bank should be apportioned among
the several counties of the State according to their
representation in the legislature. At first no limit
appears to have been placed to the amounts of a
bank's money which its president and directors
could themselves borrow. The result was that

they borrowed as much as they wished, and loaned it to their friends on such security as seemed satisfactory to themselves.

The choice of president and directors by the legislature, designed to give the people control of the bank's management, led to gross corruption and abuse, being aided greatly in these directions by the requirement for equal distribution of loans throughout the State and by the lack of any limit upon the sums which the president and directors could borrow. When the several branches had been established, each with its president and directors, there were annually to be chosen by the legislature between sixty and seventy directors. In their campaigns for election to the legislature, candidates would point to the requirement for the equal distribution of loans among the people, and promise each one of their supporters a loan in case of election. Before members who had been elected after such pledges, the candidates for bank directors had to go for election. Mr. J. H. Fitts, of Tuscaloosa,—to whose valuable paper upon the history of the State Bank and its branches, read by him before the Alabama Bankers' Association in June, 1891, we are indebted for most of the information in this article,—says the number of candidates for directors was usually two or three times as great as the number of places to be filled, adding: "For, it must be remembered, the office of bank director, without salary or any emolument whatever, was regarded by many as the most lucrative office in

the State. The legislature was annually beset by a
horde of greedy adventurers, who were candidates
for bank directors, and who resorted to all kinds
of electioneering tricks and promises to secure
their election. Unfortunately for the banks, the
votes of too many members of the legislature were
controlled by the liberality of candidates in prom-
ising bank discounts to them and their friends."
Mr. J. W. Garrett, in his "Reminiscences of Public Men in Alabama," gives an amusing incident
illustrating this abuse. A member of one branch
of the legislature died while a campaign for the
election of bank directors was in progress, and
all his fellow-members wore the usual badge of
crape on the arm for thirty days. A shrewd
countryman from a remote county, who happened
to be visiting the capital, noticing that all the men
with crape were the recipients of "treats" of all
kinds, including cigars and suppers galore, put a
similar badge upon his own arm and had a royal
good time for several days before the imposture
was discovered.

Mr. Fitts relates that one of the hotel-keepers of
Tuscaloosa succeeded in getting himself elected a
bank director in 1832. "The increased patron-
age of his hotel was wonderful; many members
of the legislature, and a great majority of the
persons who visited Tuscaloosa to borrow money,
stopped at his hotel with the view of securing the
influence of the proprietor with the Board of·
Directors, which passed upon all applications for

8

money." Four other hotel-keepers in the same city, realizing that there was no other way in which to compete with such attractions, became candidates, and in 1834 they were all elected. On one occasion when the five hotel-keepers constituted a majority of the Board of Directors, and had discounted a great many notes and bills, each note or bill receiving the ardent advocacy of one of the hotel-keepers and the votes of all five, a note was passed around which received nobody's support, and was about to be rejected, when the president, who was not in sympathy with the majority, remarked quietly of the signer of the note: "This man must have camped out last night."

Of course, members of the legislature had great influence on the directors. "No director," says Mr. Fitts, "could expect the vote of a member whose bill he refused to discount. This made it an easy matter for members of the legislature to borrow money for themselves and their friends. The directors were even afraid to refuse to discount paper which was recommended by a member of the legislature."

There could be only one outcome of such a state of affairs. The State Bank had, in 1826, a capital of $253,646 and a circulation of $273,507. In 1837 the capital of the State Bank and its branches had reached $7,889,886, and the circulation $4,576,752. The notes discounted and bills purchased in 1826 amounted to $448,859; in 1837 they amounted to $17,693,983. A commission which had been appointed, because of alleged bank frauds, to investigate the character of these notes and discounts estimated that over six millions of the $17,693,983 were worthless. This made the liabilities of the banks nearly seven millions greater than their assets, and made it plain that something heroic must be done to prevent immediate collapse. Only a year before, the people believed themselves to be enjoying boundless prosperity. They had such faith in the money of their banks that the legislature, on January 9, 1836, passed an act "abolishing direct taxation in the State," and setting aside $100,-000 of the bank money to defray the expenses of the State government. That was a practical application of the contention that if a State can create money then there is no need of taxation. The people of Alabama in this respect carried the cheap-money idea to its logical conclusion. They made the test when they were in the midst of what are known as the "flush times of Alabama." Everybody had little difficulty in getting some money into his pocket. Yet scarcely had the test begun when a panic swept over the State, and it was discovered suddenly that something was the matter with the financial and business situation. The legislature was summoned in special session to devise means of relief. The demand from all quarters was for more money for the people, and it was decided by the legislature to heed it, by authorizing the State to loan the people $5,000,000 more through the banks. This was in June. In December following, a further loan of $2,500,000 was made. These extreme measures only postponed the inevitable collapse, while adding greatly to its disastrous consequences. In 1842 the charters of the branch banks were repealed, and in 1845 that of the State Bank expired by limitation.

When the results came to be summed up, it was discovered that the University and other funds, aggregating several millions of dollars, had been lost, and that the State had sunk with them many millions more. Mr. Fitts placed the total loss to the State, principal and interest, up to June, 1891, at over $31,000,000, and estimated the amount of interest which the taxpayers are called upon annually to pay on account of the lost funds and outstanding bonds at over $271,-000 a year. In a recent speech which Governor Jones, of Alabama, made in Camden County, he placed the total amount of taxation for these objects at $362,000 a year, or nearly $1000 a day. This gives us a concrete example of the cost of cheap-money experiments which is of great value. Governor Jones used it very forcibly as a warning to his people against the insidious teachings of the advocates of the subtreasury scheme, for the latter plan in many respects resembles the Alabama plan. As Mr. Fitts well says, the Alabama experience "demonstrates the folly of a government attempting to carry on a banking business with public funds managed or controlled by its politicians."

CHAPTER XI

MISSISSIPPI'S CROP-MOVING CURRENCY

MISSISSIPPI'S experience with cheap money, during the period of inflation and speculation which followed the removal by President Jackson of the public deposits from the United States Bank, and the refusal to recharter that bank, was more reckless than that of Alabama, and consequently more disastrous. It began in 1833 and ended in 1840. For five or six years the people of Mississippi believed themselves to be the richest and most prosperous on the face of the globe. Everybody had all the money he wanted, and if he needed more the banks would pour it out for him. Yet when the end came everybody discovered that he was so poor that the State arose as one man and repudiated its most solemn obligations, thus adding breach of faith to its other follies. In this respect its conduct was in most unfavorable contrast with that of Alabama, though the disasters both suffered had been brought on by similar causes.

"Nowhere," says Professor William G. Sumner

in his " History of American Currency," in commenting upon the developments of this period, " had the paper-money mania raged worse than in Mississippi, where the banks operated as cotton factors, manufacturing money to carry cotton as they needed it." The experiment began in 1833 when the State came to the aid of the Planters' Bank of Mississippi, which had been chartered three years before, by issuing $2,000,-000 worth of bonds, at six per cent. interest, to be used as the bank's capital. The avowed object was to enable the bank to " aid in developing the resources of the State." The bonds sold at a premium, and the bank had a remarkable prosperity during the following year. This was so encouraging that nine new banks were chartered in 1834, and many others in following years. In 1838 the State, desiring to get a larger share in the general prosperity brought on by such liberal banking, chartered a bank of its own called the " Union Bank of Mississippi," and issued $5,000,-000 worth of bonds at five per cent., most of which were sold in Holland at their par value, bringing into the State the largest sum of money its people had ever dreamed of possessing. The whole State went wild with a fever of speculation. The smaller banks did their best to rival the Union Bank, and all vied with one another in pouring out currency, making loans and discounts, and publishing fabulous accounts of their prosperity.

At the close of 1839 the twenty-six banks in the State professed to have a paid-up capital of over $30,000,000, loans and discounts exceeding $48,-000,000, a note circulation exceeding $15,000,000, and deposits aggregating nearly $9,000,000. As the free white population of the State at that time was only 170,000, the alleged paid-up capital per head equaled $180, loans and discounts $285, and the circulation, including deposits, $140. Here, surely, was the largest *per capita* circulation ever known, larger by $40 than what our wildest cheap-money advocates demand now; yet what was the result? At the moment of greatest apparent prosperity, when everybody believed himself rich and hourly growing richer, the entire system collapsed. It was then discovered that all of the boasted $30,000,000 of paid-up capital, with the exception of the money that had been borrowed on the bonds of the State, consisted of "stock notes" which had been paid in for capital, the banks discounting them and the proceeds going to pay for stock subscriptions. This was simply an exchange of one form of credit for another. Absolutely no money had gone into the banks except that obtained by the sale of State bonds, and when that was exhausted nothing remained but entries upon the bank records for indebtedness from which nothing was ever to be realized.

In summing up the result, Mr. Henry V. Poor, from whose "Money, its Laws and History " we have obtained much of our information, says:

The $48,000,000 of loans were never paid; the $23,000,-000 of notes and deposits never redeemed. The whole system fell a huge and shapeless wreck, leaving the people of the State very much as they came into the world. Their condition at the time beggars description. Society was broken up from its very foundations. Everybody was in debt without any possible means of payment. Lands became worthless for the reason that no one had any money to pay for them. The only personal property left was slaves, to save which such numbers of people fled with them from the State that the common return upon legal processes was in the very abbreviated form of "G. T. T.," *gone to Texas*, a State which in this way received a mighty accession to her population.

The State paid the interest on the bonds issued for the banks for less than a year, when the governor informed the bondholders that the State, "in her sovereign capacity, had refused payment of her bonds." This position the legislature sustained in 1842 by adopting a report of a committee declaring payment of the bonds to be "incompatible with the honor and dignity of the State." The State's conduct was defended on the floor of Congress by Jacob Thompson, afterward President Buchanan's Secretary of the Interior. The bondholders had the question of the constitutionality of the bonds brought before the highest court in the State, and obtained a decision in their favor, the court affirming their constitutionality and declaring them to be binding obligations upon the State, but as no execution could issue against the State, the bondholders could obtain none of their lost money. As late as 1853 some of the bondholders, by persistent efforts, obtained from the legislature an act referring the question of payment to the people. The people voted that the bonds should not be paid, thus adding the final and overwhelming touch to the State's disgrace.

Surely there could not be found in the long and almost inexhaustible calendar of cheap-money experiments a more striking moral lesson than this Mississippi history affords; for a system which destroys not only the material prosperity of a people, but its moral sense as well, is one that should be shunned like a pestilence.

CHAPTER XII

A CHEAP-MONEY RETROSPECT

THOSE readers who have followed this series of articles upon cheap-money experiments to the present point cannot fail to have observed that we have arranged the order of the series upon a cumulative plan. We began with a plain exposition of the imperative need on the part of the people of this country of a clear conviction that no money except the best was worth the having, and that "cheap money," in any and all forms, is a delusion from which all people should pray to be delivered. From this we passed to a historical survey of the more notable of the many experiments which have been made in various countries and times to improve the condition of States and nations by making money cheap and plentiful. We propose now to recapitulate briefly the chief points in this survey in order that the full moral force of its teaching may not be missed.

We should say, perhaps, at the outset that no formal reply has been made to numerous letters

that have come to us questioning in one way or
another statements which had been advanced in
some of the earlier articles of the series, for the
reason that all the objections raised by these letters have been most effectively answered by subsequent articles. For example, when objection
was made that we took too emphatic ground in
favor of the best money and too extreme ground
against "cheap money," it seemed to us better to
show by human experience that our position was
the only safe or tenable one than to argue that it
must be so. So with other objections that the
first historical cases which we cited covered only
a part of the problems of our country to-day.
We preferred to answer these by giving further
citations which did cover the points of the prob-
lem not reached by the first.

The first historical experiment recalled by us
was that of the English Land Bank of 1696.
This was the most formidable project ever
broached for the establishment upon private capital of a bank which should lend money on land as
security. The Government granted a charter on
condition of the requisite amount of capital being
subscribed, and the King subscribed £5000 as an
example to the nation; but beyond that the Government was in no way identified with the bank.
The subscription books were opened with entire
confidence that the necessary £1,300,000 would be
obtained within a few days. At the end of the
period allowed for raising it only £2100 had been

subscribed by the entire nation. It was thus shown that private capital was not eager to enter into the business of lending money on land. The country gentlemen, who had been eager for the establishment of the bank, were not in position to subscribe to its capital, since their sole purpose in wishing for it was to be able to borrow money from it on their land, and, wishing to borrow, they of course were not able to lend. The capitalists would not put their money into it because its avowed object was to injure them by lowering the rate of interest and lessening the demand for existing money. The result was complete failure to establish the bank.

Passing from this failure of 1696, we took up a notable attempt which was made in Rhode Island about a century later to establish a Land Bank as a State institution, which should lend money on land as security, and pledge the faith of the State for its redemption. We showed that from the outset this experiment was a failure; that the money which the State declared to be a legal tender for public and private debts never circulated at par, but was depreciated from its first issue; that it paralyzed the industries and commerce of the State; that the whole power of the State government was not sufficient to make it circulate at par; that it led to the repudiation of the greater part of the State debt, giving Rhode Island the name of "Rogues' Island" throughout the land; that it dropped steadily during the three years of the bank's existence till one dollar in coin was worth fifteen of the Land Bank issue, and that the end was a collapse of credit and business so complete that years were required for the State to recover from it.

Criticism was made upon our citation of the Rhode Island experiment that it was attempted in a small and struggling State, at the close of the exhausting Revolutionary War, and that it could not be taken as a criterion of what would be the outcome were the United States Government to go into the business of loaning money on land. It was argued that the wealth of this mighty and prosperous nation was so great, as compared with the resources of Rhode Island, that any attempt to make the experience of one apply to the other was absurd. As an answer to this objection we cited the famous John Law experiment in France in 1718. This was the Rhode Island principle applied to a great nation, and, as a basis for its operation, the entire property of the nation was brought into the bank and used as security for its loans. Law's idea was to have all France as a mortgage, and he carried out the idea to its fullest extent. Only two years were necessary for him to lead the nation at a headlong gallop to overwhelming disaster, in which all credit was destroyed, all industrial values ruined, and everything except landed property left worthless.

Finally, lest some critics might say that all

9

these unsuccessful attempts had been made in times long past, and under different economic and industrial and commercial conditions from those which obtain in our own time, we took up the case of the Argentine Republic, giving in much detail the efforts of that country to obtain prosperity under the same system of finance that had failed in Rhode Island and in France. That it was the same system was recognized in Buenos Ayres by sound financial thinkers, who opposed its adoption. After our article on Law's experiment was in press, and the article upon the Argentine experience had been completed, we found in the "Buenos Ayres Standard" an editorial article upon John Law from which we quote the following passages:

The calamity brought on France by John Law was the most tremendous that can be imagined; it has no parallel in history except the present crisis in Buenos Ayres. But in many respects Law's crisis was less disastrous than that which has now commenced in our city, the outcome of which nobody can venture to predict.

If Argentine statesmen really believe that they can issue notes at will, they will find that they are sadly mistaken. We must come, some day, to a grand wind-up, and the convulsion that must ensue will eclipse anything before seen in the world. Men and women will go mad in the streets, and no government will be able to face the hurricane of popular indignation.

We cannot resist the wish to send all our shinplaster advocates to Venice, to end their days in obscurity, like Law.

It is only fair to Law's memory to say that he admitted the error of his theories before his death, and regarded shinplasters as a calamity of the greatest magnitude.

We then showed that the subtreasury scheme of the Farmers' Alliance was more dangerous than Law's because the money which it called for would be issued upon a far less certain and stable foundation of values than his plan provided. The *per capita* delusion, which lies at the foundation of all cheap-money experiments, was then discussed in the light of the revelations and demonstrations made in foregoing chapters, for the purpose of showing how utterly mistaken it is. Michigan experience with "wild-cat banks" between 1837 and 1840, Alabama's experiment in free banking with State funds for capital between 1825 and 1842, and Mississippi's experiment of similar character between 1833 and 1840 were the subjects of our next chapters. Like all other cheap-money experiments, these ended in disaster. In every case the final result has been ruin, and the wider the field of trial, the more desolating has been the calamity. The Argentine Republic believed itself an exceptional nation, rich and powerful enough to change this unbroken current of human experience, but its people know now how terribly mistaken they were. We do not believe it possible that the American people will ever be capable of such folly.

CHAPTER XIII

THE PEOPLE'S MONEY

WHAT is the best kind of money for the people—using the latter word in the sense in which it is employed by the advocates of free silver coinage? These advocates, like the champions of all other forms of cheap money during the past three centuries, speak of gold as the money of the rich, of bankers and money-lenders, of capitalists and rich corporations, whom they denominate " gold-bugs," and whose center of activity is Wall street. All the remaining elements of the population are classed together as "the people," to whom, it is now claimed, free silver is the money which would bring the largest measure of prosperity and happiness. Is this claim well founded; or is it, like all other alleged cheap-money benefits, a delusion founded partly upon ignorance of economic laws and principles, and partly upon private and personal greed?

The silver dollar which the free-coinage advocates desire to have bestowed upon the people is

one containing 371¼ grains of pure silver, worth
in the markets of the world, at the present writing, about 70 cents. The proposition is that the
United States shall take this amount of silver,
coin it free of charge, stamp it "one dollar," and
make it a legal tender for all public and private
debts. That means that the United States shall
pay $1.29 an ounce for silver, in any and all
amounts from any and every quarter, though the
market price is only 90 cents an ounce, and shall
make payment in legal-tender money intercon-
vertible with gold at par.

What would be the first effect of the passage
of this law? There is not an economist of any
standing anywhere in the world who will not say
that the first effect would be the disappearance of
gold entirely from our circulation, and the de-
scent of the country to the silver standard. The
silver advocates claim that the mere passage of
the law would force the price of silver from 90
cents up to $1.29 an ounce, but there is no possi-
bility of such an effect. They claim that silver
has fallen in value because of its demonetization
by nearly all the nations of the world, whereas
the real cause is an enormous increase in production, and great improvements in mining, by which
the cost of production has been diminished. The
yearly average product of silver from 1851 to
1875 was $51,000,000, and from 1876 to 1890 it
was $116,000,000, an increase of 127 per cent.
The yearly average product of gold between 1851

and 1875 was $127,000,000, and between 1876 and
1890 $108,000,000, a decrease of 15 per cent. That
is why gold has more than maintained its value,
while silver has depreciated. In 1873 silver was,
worth $1.30 an ounce, in 1874 it had dropped
to $1.27, in 1875 to $1.24, and in 1876 to $1.15.
In 1877 a free-coinage bill was introduced in
Congress, and in 1878 it was amended so as to
provide for the coinage of not less than two million nor more than four million dollars' worth of
silver bullion per month into dollars to be full
legal tender at their nominal value. This was
passed, vetoed by President Hayes, and passed
over his veto. It was claimed that this would
raise the price of silver. Since it became a law
405,000,000 silver dollars have been coined, 348,-
000,000 of which are locked up in the Treasury
vaults, never having passed into circulation. The
price of silver dropped to $1.12 an ounce in 1879,
reached $1.14 in 1880, $1.13 in 1881 and 1882, fell
to $1.11 in 1883, to 99 cents in 1886, to 93½ cents
in 1889, and to 90 cents in 1892. In 1890 Congress enacted a law which authorized the Secretary of the Treasury to purchase four and a half
million ounces of silver bullion per month at the
market price, and to give in return for it legal-
tender notes redeemable in gold or silver at the
option of the Government. Even this enforced
purchase of 54,000,000 ounces of silver a year has
not stayed the downward progress of the price.

A striking demonstration of the utter folly

of the claim that free coinage would lift the price of silver from 90 cents to $1.29 an ounce is made by Mr. Louis R. Ehrich, of Colorado Springs, to whose luminous and valuable work, "The Question of Silver," we are indebted for much exact information. At the time he wrote silver was 95 cents an ounce, but his demonstration is none the less effective. He says:

There is on our planet, in round figures, three billion nine hundred million dollars' worth of silver held as money or as a fund for money redemption. That is to-day all worth about 95 cents an ounce. Now these free-silver men tell us that the natural alchemy of free coinage by the United States all alone is going to raise these thirty-nine hundred millions from 95 cents to $1.29. That is, it is going to add a value of over a billion dollars to the world's silver stock. Astonishing proposition!

All authorities agree that the silver of the world would be dumped almost in a body upon us, at the advanced coinage price which our Government would have to pay till we abandoned the gold standard, or gold went to a premium, which would be in a very short time after the law went into operation. We should then have only one kind of money, a dollar worth 70 cents, which every man who had a debt the payment of which was not stipulated to be in gold, could use to pay off 100 cents' worth of debt, and which every man who earned money in any way would have to receive for 100 cents' worth of work. All debts · would therefore be scaled down 30 per cent., except those with a gold-payment stipulation, and all wages, pensions, salaries, life-insurance policies, and savings-bank deposits would be cut down in the same way. There would be no escape. The dear money, gold, would be driven out of circulation by the cheaper money, silver, by the working of a law as inexorable as the law of gravitation.

Attention was called to this effect upon the pensioners of the Government in a circular which Congressman Harter, of Ohio, sent to all the Grand Army Posts a few weeks ago. In that he said:

If a *Free-Silver Bill* becomes law, a veteran who now gets a pension worth to him $4.00 per month would receive *actually* but $2.80, with the chance of it going down to an actual value of $2.40. Take the case of a soldier who is a total physical wreck and utterly unable to do for himself. Such a man gets $72.00 per month. If a Free-Silver Bill passes, while he would *nominally* get the same, he would really get but $50.40, with a strong probability that in the early future his $72.00 of monthly pension would be worth not over $43.20. This coinage question should not be one of party politics. It rises above partizanship. The honor of the country is at stake. Its business interests from ocean to ocean and from lake to gulf are jeopardized. Its good faith not only to its living soldiers is brought in question, but if a so-called free-coinage bill becomes law, the widows and orphans of the nation's dead will be robbed by the laws of the land they died to save. The law would work a monstrous wrong, for from the moment it goes upon the statute book it represents over $45,000,000 per year taken from the ex-soldiers, their widows, and their orphans.

That would be the effect upon the pensioners, without a doubt. No man who has a rudimentary knowledge of economic laws can question that for a moment. Let us see what would be the effect upon savings-bank deposits and life-insurance policies.

There are deposited in our savings-banks sixteen hundred millions of dollars, a sum greater than the entire amount of money in active circulation in this country. These deposits are for the most part made up of small amounts, and represent the savings of the working-classes. Of these savings a thousand millions are invested in mortgages. Many of these mortgages are made payable in gold, but many others are not. Every one of them which has not a gold-paying clause can be paid off in silver; that is, the holder of it can be compelled to receive $700 as full payment for every $1000 of money lent. Is this honest or wise? Would a man who paid his honest debts in that way ever be able to secure another loan? Every mortgage in future would bear a gold-paying clause, and it would be very difficult to induce lenders who had been cheated once to trust the persons who had cheated them with a further loan on any terms.

Who are the lenders who would be cheated if mortgage indebtedness were to be paid in silver at 70 cents on a dollar? Are they "gold-bugs"? On the contrary, in many cases they are widows and orphans who are living on the hard earnings of industrious people, saved through many years of economy and toil. The "gold-bugs" have been merely the agents for the investment of this money, seeking for it a sure and safe return to the people who have put it in their care. The indispensable requisite for such return is the most sure and unvarying standard of value known to man—that is, the gold standard. The "gold-bug" who insists upon that is the truest possible friend and servant of the people, whether he be acting as their agent in lending them money, or investing and caring for it at the head of an insurance company, or in any other capacity. Rich men do not lend money; they borrow it—borrow it from the banks and insurance companies to invest it for their profit, and for the profit of its owners. They are the agents for all the money-savers of the land, seeking to win for them the best income possible upon their savings. They place the mortgages upon the western farms, and upon the buildings and other property in western cities, and the money which they use for that purpose is the money which the people, the workers and savers of the land, place in banks and insurance companies for their families and for use in their hour of need.

These are the people who would suffer by the swindle of making 70 cents do the work of a dollar by process of law. Every working-man in the land, every person drawing a salary, would suffer in the same way. He would receive the same number of dollars as before, but each dollar would buy only 70 cents' worth of commodities. He is in fact a creditor for every day's or every week's work, and he is cheated of more than a third of his earnings if, when pay-day comes around, he must take $7 in place of $10, or $14 in place of $20.

The true "people's money" is the best money; that is, the money which will buy the most of what every man needs, and which will be worth the same this week as it was last, the same next year as this year. There is no security for savings of any kind with any other standard of value, no safety for loans, no interest on bank deposits. The man who declares cheap money in any form to be the "people's money" is the worst possible enemy of the people, for his policy, if carried out by the Government, would rob the people of a large portion of their hard-earned savings; would cut down their wages, and would throw the whole business of the country into confusion and doubt, sending paralysis and disaster into every industry and into every branch of trade and commerce. The worst sufferers would be the toilers of all kinds, the people of moderate means, and the poor. If the advocates of free coinage were honest in their contention that the country's welfare would be enhanced by having both silver and gold as a basis for its currency, they would consent to the coinage of a silver dollar worth 100 cents; but this they refuse to do.

They refuse to accept an honest dollar, and insist upon a dishonest dollar. They are not serving the people, but are serving the devil, and the issue which they raise, far from being a political one, is a moral one of the first magnitude.

CHAPTER XIV[1]

THE FRENCH ASSIGNATS AND MANDATS

IT would have been reasonable to suppose that the experience which France had with cheap money under John Law's guidance in the early part of the eighteenth century, described in Chapter V of this book, would have imparted a lesson not soon to be forgotten. But such was not the case. Before the end of the century a new and not dissimilar experiment was made in the same direction, ending, like its predecessor, in failure and almost boundless confusion and disaster.

One of the first and most serious troubles which confronted the republic established by the French Revolution of 1789, was the scarcity of money. This was due to many causes, but chiefly, says Thiers, to the "want of confidence occasioned by the disturbances." The same authority adds the following general truth about circulation, which is applicable to all countries and in all times:

[1] This chapter was not included in the pamphlet edition of this publication. It has been added in order to make the collection more nearly complete.

"Specie is apparent by the circulation. When confidence prevails, the activity of exchange is extreme; money moves about rapidly, is seen everywhere, and is believed to be more considerable because it is more serviceable; but when political commotions create alarm, capital languishes, specie moves slowly; it is frequently hoarded, and complaints are unjustly made of its absence." To increase the supply of circulating medium, it was proposed that the National Assembly issue paper money based on the church lands which had been confiscated by the Government. These lands were yielding no revenue, but were a heavy burden. The money, to be called assignats, was really a form of titles to the confiscated lands; for it was receivable in payment for them, and was designed, in addition to furnishing revenue to the government, to bring about a distribution of those lands among the people. The debates of the National Assembly upon the proposition showed that John Law's experiment had not been entirely forgotten. There was strong opposition, but it was overcome by arguments that bear a curious resemblance to some which are heard in our day in favor of various forms of cheap money which are advocated for the United States. "Paper money," said one of the advocates of the assignats, "under a despotism is dangerous; it favors corruption; but in a nation constitutionally governed, which takes care of its own notes, which determines their number and use, that danger no longer exists." How like that is to the argument heard here, and in the Argentine Republic as well, that a great and rich and prosperous and free nation could make its own economic laws, invent its own monetary systems, and even defy the teachings of all other nations with entire safety! These curious arguments carried the day in the National Assembly, and a first issue of assignats, to the value of 400,000,000 francs, was issued in December, 1789. They bore interest and were made payable at sight, but no interest was ever paid, and subsequent issues had no interest provision. The first issue represented about one fifth of the total value of the confiscated lands.

Yet with this solid basis of value upon which to rest, the assignats never circulated at par. A few months after the first issue demands began to be made for a second issue, as is invariably the case in all experiments of this kind. Talleyrand opposed the second issue in a speech of great ability, many of whose passages have passed into economic literature as model statements of funda-mental monetary principles. "The assignat," he said, "considered as a title of credit, has a positive and material value; this value of the assignat is precisely the same as that of the land which it represents; but still it must be admitted, above all, that never will any national paper be upon a par with the metals; never will the supplementary sign of the first representative sign of wealth have the exact value of its model; *the very title proves want, and want spreads alarm and distrust around it.*" And again: "You can arrange it so that people shall be forced to take a thousand francs in paper for a thousand francs in specie, but you never can arrange it so that the people shall be obliged to give a thousand francs in specie for a thousand francs in paper." Still again: "Assignat money, however safe, however solid it may be, is an abstraction of paper money; it is consequently but the free or forced sign, not of wealth, but merely of credit." In answer to the arguments of Talleyrand, the most effective, because most "taking" argument, if argument it can be called, was the following by Mirabeau: "It is in vain to compare assignats, secured on the solid basis of these domains, to an ordinary paper currency possessing a forced circulation. They represent real property, the most secure of all possessions, the land on which we tread."

The advocates of money based on lands who are heard in our country to-day will recognize their own doctrine in this resounding phrase of Mirabeau. It carried the day in the National Assembly, and in September, 1790, a second issue of assignats, to the value of 800,000,000 francs, bearing no interest, was ordered.

The decree for this second issue contained a pledge that in no case should the amount of assignats exceed twelve hundred millions. But the nation was drunk with its own stimulant, and pledges were of no value. In June, 1791, a third issue of 600,000,000 was ordered. This was followed soon afterward by a fourth issue of 300,-000,000, and by a new pledge that the total amount should never be allowed to exceed sixteen hundred millions. But this pledge, like two others that had been made before it, was broken as soon as a demand for more issues became irresistible. Fresh issues followed each other in rapid succession in 1792, and at the close of that year an official statement was put forth that a total of thirty-four hundred millions had been issued, of which six hundred millions had been destroyed, leaving twenty-eight hundred millions in circulation.

Specie had disappeared from circulation soon after the second issue, and the value of the assignats began to go steadily and rapidly downward. Business and industry soon felt the effects, and the inevitable collapse followed. Ex-President Andrew D. White, whose tract, "Paper Money Inflation in France," is the most admirable and complete statement of this experience which has been published, says of the situation at this stage:

What the bigotry of Louis XIV, and the shiftlessness of Louis XV, could not do in nearly a century, was accomplished by this tampering with the currency in a few months. Everything that tariffs and custom-houses could do was done. Still the great manufactories of Normandy were closed; those of the rest of the kingdom speedily followed, and vast numbers of workmen, in all parts of the country, were thrown out of employment.

In the spring of 1791 no one knew whether a piece of

paper money, representing 100 francs, would, a month later, have a purchasing power of 100 francs, or 90 francs, or 80, or 60. The result was that capitalists declined to embark their means in business. Enterprise received a mortal blow. Demand for labor was still further diminished. The business of France dwindled into a mere living from hand to mouth. This state of things, too, while it bore heavily against the interests of the moneyed classes, was still more ruinous to those in more moderate, and most of all to those in straitened circumstances. With the masses of the people the purchase of every article of supply became a speculation: a speculation in which the professional speculator had an immense advantage over the buyer. Says the most brilliant apologist for French Revolutionary statesmanship, "Commerce was dead, betting took its place."

In the early part of 1792 the assignat was 30 per cent. below par. In the following year it had fallen to 67 per cent. below par. A basis for further issues was secured by the confiscation of lands of emigrant nobles, and a flood of assignats poured forth upon the country in steadily increasing volume. Before the close of 1794 seven thousand millions had been issued, and the year 1796 opened with a total issue of forty-five thousand millions, of which thirty-six thousand millions were in actual circulation. By February of that year the total issue had advanced to 45,500,000,000, and the value had dropped to one two-hundred-and-sixty-fifth part of their nominal value. A note professing to be worth about $20 of our money was worth about 6 cents.

The Government now came forward with a new

scheme, offering to redeem the assignats, on the basis of 30 to 1, for mandats — a new form of paper money, which entitled the holder to take immediate possession, at their estimated value, of any of the lands pledged by the assignats. Eight hundred millions in mandats were issued, to be exchanged for the assignats, and the plates for printing the latter were destroyed. Six hundred millions more of mandats were issued for the public service. At first the mandats circulated at as high as 80 per cent. of their nominal value, but additional issues sent them down in value even more rapidly than the assignats had fallen, and in a very short time they were worth only one thousandth part of their nominal value. It was evident that the end had come. Before the assignats were withdrawn, the Government resorted to various expedients to hold up their value by legislative decrees. The use of coin was prohibited; a maximum price in assignats was fixed for commodities by law; the purchase of specie was forbidden under penalty of imprisonment in irons for six years; and the sale of assignats below their nominal value was forbidden under penalty of imprisonment for twenty years in chains. Investment of capital in foreign countries was punishable with death. All these efforts were as futile as similar efforts had been in John Law's time. The value of the assignats went steadily down. Bread-riots broke out in Paris, and the Government was compelled to supply the capital with provisions. When the mandats fell as the assignats had fallen before them, the Government was convinced that it was useless to try to give value to valueless paper by simply printing more paper and calling it by another name; and on July 1, 1796, it swept away the whole mass by issuing a decree authorizing everybody to transact business in any money he chose. "No sooner," says Mr. McLeod, in his "Economical Philosophy," "was this great blow struck at the paper currency, of making it pass at its current value, than specie immediately reappeared in circulation." In commenting upon this second experience of France with paper money, which lasted for about six years, Prof. A. L. Perry, in his "Elements of Political Economy," thus graphically and truthfully sums up the consequences:

The distress and consternation into which a country falls when its current Measure of Services is disturbed and destroyed, as it was in this case, is past all powers of description. The prisons and the guillotine did not compare with the assignats in causing suffering during those six years. This example is significant because it shows the powerlessness of even the strongest and most unscrupulous governments to regulate the value of anything. The assignats were depreciating during the very months in which Robespierre and the Committee of Public Safety were wielding the power of life and death in France with terrific energy. They did their utmost to stop the sinking of the Revolutionary paper. But value knows its own laws, and follows them in spite of decrees and penalties.

CHAPTER XV

ANOTHER WORD ON "CHEAP MONEY"

WITH the failure of the free-coinage bill in Congress, the danger that this country might be called upon to pass through the quagmire of a fresh cheap-money experiment seems to have been averted, for the present surely, and in all probability for a long time to come. It is apparent now that whatever of popular sentiment there may have been behind the free-silver movement at its beginning, there was very little behind it at the time of the free-coinage bill's failure, and even less at this moment than there was then. The American people have always shown great quickness in educating themselves on financial and economic questions, and the sudden subsidence of the free-silver "craze" shows that the work of education, so far as that form of cheap money is concerned, has been practically accomplished.

The Century rejoices sincerely in the assurances which have come to it from many sources that its efforts to assist in this work of education

117

have not been unsuccessful. Now that the work is ended for the present, it may not be amiss, in taking leave of the subject, to quote a few striking passages, on the evils of cheap money, from the writings of two masters of vigorous English who studied different phases of those evils in former times. The truth of their forcible language will be all the more appreciated now, since we are coming more and more each day to a proper realization of the perils from which, as a nation, we have had so narrow an escape.

In 1722 one William Wood, a hardware merchant, obtained from the British crown a patent to coin copper money for Ireland to the amount of £108,000. He had no power to compel any one to take his halfpence, which he coined under this grant and sent to Ireland; and when a large batch of them arrived there the people refused to take and use them as money. They were made of such base metal, and were so much smaller than the English halfpence, that they were worth in gold or silver not more than a twelfth of their face-value. When the Irish people refused to accept them as money, there was talk of Wood's obtaining orders from the crown compelling the king's commissioners and collectors of customs in Ireland to take them as money, and thus force them into circulation. Upon this proposition, Dean Swift, then in the full vigor of his wonderful powers as a controversialist, published a series of pamphlets or letters addressed to the tradesmen, shopkeepers, farmers, and common people in general, on the subject of the debased coin, which made a powerful impression in both England and Ireland, and hastened the repeal of Wood's patent. These letters were signed "Drapier," and are known in the collections of Swift's works under that title. We shall make a few quotations from them with a view to showing how perfectly his arguments against the folly of debased or cheap money, made 170 years ago, apply to the proposal to inflict upon the American people a debased silver dollar worth only 70 cents.

It was urged in defense of Wood's money that copper halfpence were scarce in Ireland; that the people needed more copper money for the transaction of their business; and that if the supply were greater everybody would be more prosperous. All that sounds very familiar. It was also said, in answer to a query as to whether Wood would keep his coinage within the £108,000 limit, that he would be guided in that respect by the "exigencies of trade." That phrase also sounds very familiar. Here is what Swift says on that point:

Wood proposes that he will not coin above £40,000 unless the exigencies of trade require it: First, I observe that this sum of £40,000 is almost double to what I proved to be sufficient for the whole kingdom, although we had not one of our old halfpence left. Again I ask, who is to be judge when the exigencies of trade require it? Without doubt ˙ he means himself, for as to us of this poor kingdom, who must be utterly ruined if his project should succeed, we were never once consulted till the matter was over, and he will judge of our exigencies by his own; neither will these be ever at an end till he and his accomplices will think they have enough.

In reference to the effects of cheap halfpence on the people of Ireland, Swift said:

Mr. Wood will never be at rest but coin on: so that in some years we shall have at least five times four score and ten thousand pounds of this lumber. Now the current money of this kingdom is not reckoned to be above four hundred thousand pounds in all; and while there is a silver sixpence, these blood-suckers will never be quiet. When once the kingdom is reduced to such a condition I will tell you what must be the end: The gentlemen of estates will all turn off their tenants for want of payment, because the tenants are obliged by their leases to pay sterling, which is lawful current money of England; then they will turn their own farmers, run all into sheep where they can, keeping only such other cattle as are necessary; then they will be their own merchants, and send their wool and butter and hides and linen beyond sea for ready money and wines and spices and silks. The farmers must rob or beg or leave the county. The shopkeepers in this and every other town must break and starve, for it is the landed man that maintains the merchant, and shopkeeper, and handicrafts-man. I should never have done, if I were to tell you all the miseries that we shall undergo if we be so foolish and wicked as to take this cursed coin. . . . In short, those halfpence are like the accursed thing, which, as the Scripture tells us, the children of Israel were forbidden to touch; they will run about like the plague and destroy everyone who lays his hands upon them.

Carlyle, in his "French Revolution," uses scarcely less vigorous, and even more picturcsque, language in regard to the *assignats* which were issued in France between 1789 and 1796. These were in the form of paper money, based at first upon the security of confiscated church lands, and afterward upon all the national domains and other property. They were issued to the amount of over forty-five billion francs, and before they were withdrawn depreciated to less than one three-hundredth of their face-value. Carlyle records that a hackney-coachman in Paris demanded six thousand livres, about fifteen hundred dollars, as fare for a short ride, in the last days of the *assignats*. In regard to the first issue, he says in the first volume of the " French Revolution ":

Wherefore, on the 19th day of December, a paper-money of *"Assignats,"* of Bonds secured, or *assigned*, on that Clerico-National Property, and unquestionably at least in payment of that,— is decreed: the first of a long series of like financial performances, which shall astonish mankind. So that now, while old rags last, there shall be no lack of circulating medium: whether of commodities to circulate thereon is another question. But, after all, does not this assignat business speak volumes for modern science ? Bankruptcy, we may say, was come, as the *end* of all Delusions needs must come: yet how gently, in softening diffusion, in mild succession, was it hereby made to fall; — like no all-destroying avalanche; like gentle showers of a powdery impalpable snow, shower after shower, till all was indeed buried, and yet little was destroyed that could not be replaced, be dispensed with ! To such length has modern machinery reached. Bankruptcy we said was great; but indeed Money itself is a standing miracle.

11

The miracle of the *assignats* consisted in creating what appeared to be something out of nothing; but it returned in due season to nothing, leaving ruin and desolation behind it.